Literature in Perspective

General Editor: Kenneth H. Grose

Chaucer

Literature in Perspective

Chaucer

M. W. Grose

Evans Brothers Limited, London

Published by Evans Brothers Limited
Montague House, Russell Square, London, W.C.1
© M. W. Grose 1967
First published 1967

Set in 11 on 12 point Bembo and printed in Great Britain by
The Camelot Press Ltd., London and Southampton
7/5281   44571   PR4167

Literature in Perspective

Of recent years, the ordinary man who reads for pleasure has been gradually excluded from that great debate in which every intelligent reader of the classics takes part. There are two reasons for this: first, so much criticism floods from the world's presses that no one but a scholar living entirely among books can hope to read it all; and second, the critics and analysts, mostly academics, use a language that only their fellows in the same discipline can understand.

Consequently criticism, which should be as 'inevitable as breathing'—an activity for which we are all qualified—has become the private field of a few warring factions who shout their unintelligible battle cries to each other but make little communication to the common man.

Literature in Perspective aims at giving a straightforward account of literature and of writers—straightforward both in content and in language. Critical jargon is as far as possible avoided; any terms that must be used are explained simply; and the constant preoccupation of the authors of the Series is to be lucid.

It is our hope that each book will be easily understood, that it will adequately describe its subject without pretentiousness so that the intelligent reader who wants to know about Donne or Keats or Shakespeare will find enough in it to bring him up to date on critical estimates.

Even those who are well read, we believe, can benefit from a lucid exposition of what they may have taken for granted, and perhaps—dare it be said?—not fully understood.

K. H. G.

Chaucer

The farther away from us in time or even space an author is, the more need there is to find out about how people round him live and think. This is why I have given what may at first sight appear a disproportionate amount of space to preliminary matter: those who disagree are welcome to skip the first half of the book, but they may find that the later chapters take for granted what has been explained in the earlier ones. A short cut is not always the quickest way home.

If this were a work of scholarship, there ought to appear here a long list of those to whom I am indebted in the writing of this book. Those whose ideas I have plundered are so numerous, nor might they be pleased to accept the paternity of the ideas expressed within these covers, that I have instead used this space for a note on the text. I hope that those who find that they have been used will accept my sincere thanks and apologies for what I have done with their own work.

All quotations from Chaucer's works are taken from the edition of his works by F. N. Robinson, 2nd ed. 1957. This is the standard modern text. It does, however, differ from all other modern editions in the order in which the *Canterbury Tales* are printed. In giving references I have therefore added in parentheses the older line numbers, where these differ, for the convenience of those who are using other editions. I have not indicated the group letter which these use where Robinson has a Roman numeral.

M. W. G.

Contents

The Author

M. W. Grose, M.A., is Senior Research Associate at the
University of Newcastle upon Tyne.

Acknowledgements

The author and publishers are indebted to the Trustees of the British Museum for permission to reproduce the cover portrait and the miniature of the Tower of London; the Walker Art Gallery, Liverpool, for the outside panels of the Aachen altarpiece and the National Gallery for the centre panel.

I

Chaucer's Life

> Whan that Aprill with his shoures soote   *sweet*
> The droghte of March hath perced to the roote,
> And bathed every veyne in swich licour   *such*
> Of which vertu engendred is the flour;   *power*
> Whan Zephirus eek with his sweete breeth
> Inspired hath in every holt and heeth   *quickened*
> The tendre croppes, and the yonge sonne
> Hath in the Ram his halve cours yronne,
> And smale foweles maken melodye,
> That slepen al the nyght with open ye
> (So priketh hem nature in hir corages);   *stirs   hearts*
> Thanne longen folk to goon on pilgrimages,
> And palmeres for to seken straunge strondes,   *pilgrims*
> To ferne halwes, kowthe in sondry londes;   *distant shrines*
> And specially from every shires ende
> Of Engelond to Caunterbury they wende,
> The hooly blisful martir for to seke,
> That hem hath holpen whan that they were seeke.
>
> CANTERBURY TALES, GENERAL PROLOGUE I, 1–18

These are the opening lines of the account of the most famous journey in English Literature made by a band of pilgrims to the shrine of St. Thomas à Becket at Canterbury. It is springtime: the birds are singing and the earth is growing green once more. It is the springtime of English Literature also, for thus begin the *Canterbury Tales* of Geoffrey Chaucer, courtier and poet, who lived in the 14th century. To Spenser (who came 200 years later, in the time of Shakespeare) he was 'that renowned Poet . . . well of English undefiled'; to others, the father of English poetry. He is, in fact, the earliest major English poet who is still read today, and he is still read for the sake of his poetry, not merely as a source book of social history.

But almost 600 years have passed since those pilgrims set out on that April morning from the Tabard Inn at Southwark; we modern readers who want to follow in their footsteps and read of what they did and said on their journey need to make a journey ourselves to take our minds back to the atmosphere of the 14th century in order to recapture the way people then lived and thought, if we are to make the most of the poem. For, while it is possible to go so far in the necessary scholarly labour of grubbing up sources that the finished product of the poet's imagination is forgotten, yet there is a certain minimum required before his poems can speak for themselves to our ears.

So let us take a look at the pilgrims and see how they lived and what was their place in society: then at their picture of the universe and the physical world around them; at the world of books and learning; at the language they spoke and how Chaucer used it in his verse. Finally, let us take a look at as many of his other works as space will permit; for if we put them in perspective among themselves and the times in which they were written they will mean more to our 20th-century minds and give us greater satisfaction. And this, after all, is why we read.

But we must start with Chaucer himself, for out of his mind all these other pilgrims came, nor is a poet's life without interest for the understanding of his poetry, even if many of the details essential for a biography of a modern figure cannot be supplied. We do not even know the exact date of his birth. The death of a famous man rarely goes unrecorded; his birth is quite another matter, for his future fame is apparent only to the doting parents. Furthermore, few biographies and private letters have come down to us from the medieval period. People preserved their business records, not their private letters. Account books such as the one in which Chaucer's name first appears can be made to yield a framework of facts, but no personal detail or gossip-column scandal. This particular account book, dating from 1357, is that for the household of Elizabeth, Countess of Ulster, the wife of the third son of King Edward III. The entry for 4 April

1357 merely records a payment to a London tailor of four shillings for a cloak, and another three shillings for a pair of red and black breeches and a pair of shoes for Geoffrey Chaucer. The precise statement of the day and the enumeration of the merchandise make the entry seem more useful than it really is. But all the same, we can tell that Chaucer must have been a page in Elizabeth's household, and that he was probably in his early teens: at any rate he was not full-grown, because clothing for a full-grown man would have cost much more. We can now place his birth around 1344: confirmation of this comes later, when in 1386 in evidence in a lawsuit he stated his age as 'forty years and more'.

In 1359, two years after this first mention, Chaucer was in France as a Squire. Edward III led a great military operation which was turned back near Rheims, where Chaucer was taken prisoner. The royal accounts show that the King paid £16 towards his ransom, or rather less than for his favourite horse. The expedition was part of the Hundred Years' War between England and France, which had already lasted thirty-three years and was to continue off and on from 1337 to 1453. The fortunes of the two sides fluctuated considerably. The first period of English supremacy was just coming to an end, and the position of the English King after the victory of Crécy in 1346, the capture of Calais in 1347 and the Black Prince's victory and capture of King John of France in 1357, was not surpassed until the reign of Henry V in the next century.

It was from such military operations that the Knight of the *Canterbury Tales* was returning when he joined the pilgrims. The wide experience of war that this 'worthy man' had undergone was typical of his class. In the middle of the 14th century, as may be seen in the foregoing paragraph, he would have been engaged in fighting for his own King in 'his lordes werre'; but when he was not needed for purely patriotic duties he would fight as a mercenary for other Christian kings in western Europe's permanent struggle against the Turks. As Chaucer says:

At Alisaundre he was whan it was wonne.   *taken*
Ful ofte tyme he hadde the bord bigonne   *sat at the head of the table*

Aboven alle nacions in Pruce;
In Lettow hadde he reysed and in Ruce,   *travelled*
No Cristen man so ofte of his degree.
In Gernade at the seege eek hadde he be
Of Algezir, and riden in Belmarye.
At Lyeys was he and at Satalye,
Whan they were wonne; and in the Grete See
At many a noble armee hadde he be.   *armed expedition*
At mortal batailles hadde he been fiftene,
And foughten for oure feith at Tramyssene
In lystes thries, and ay slayn his foo.   *tournament*
This ilke worthy knyght hadde been also   *same*
Somtyme with the lord of Palatye
Agayn another hethen in Turkye.
And evermoore he hadde a sovereyn prys. . . .

CT: GEN. PROL. I, 51-67

Eastern Europe and the Middle East are studded with impreg-
nable fortresses, such as the Krak des Chevaliers in Syria, where
he and his like would spend the months in between their cam-
paigns, and indulge in the tourneyings and joustings, the Courts
of Love (see pp. 102–6) and the general high life of the age. But
though Chaucer idealizes this 'verray parfit gentil knyght',
chivalry was already on the decline, and his main business was
war, an expensive and dangerous pastime, even if it often does
seem to us now to resemble rather an elaborate game of cricket.

The Hundred Years' War was a serious drain on the royal fin-
ances throughout its course. It was the reason for the heavy taxation in 1377–81 which led to the Peasants' Revolt (see pp.
22–23). Yet despite his debts, the Court of Edward III was one
of the most splendid in Europe; at one time, two other kings,
John of France and David of Scotland, were there as honoured
prisoners. The next record of Chaucer, seven years later, shows
that in 1367 when he was in his early twenties he was at the Royal
Court holding the posts, first of Yeoman, then of Squire. What he
was doing in the intervening years nobody knows for certain,
though a 16th-century tradition has it that he studied law at the
Inner Temple, one of the Inns of Court, where he was fined two

shillings for brawling with a Franciscan friar in Fleet Street. The records which might have proved this are now lost, but the story has been traced back to one of their keepers, which gives it authority, and certainly his later career points strongly to a sound knowledge of law.

The Squires in great households may light-heartedly be described as the equivalent of Bertie Wooster's Jeeves. The rule books for the households of Edward II (1307–27) (the father of Edward III), and of Edward IV (1461–83) still exist, and from them we can see something of the duties which would have come Chaucer's way. Edward II had three 'Esquires for the Kinges Chamber', who were his constant companions, night and day, and who would dress and undress him and see to his other wants. Of a lower rank there were a larger number of Squires of the Household: Chaucer was one of these. Edward IV had an establishment of fifty of these Squires, but his household was smaller than Edward II's. At Christmas 1367 there were thirty-six who were entitled to new robes, and Chaucer's name is seventeenth on the list. Edward IV's rule book says that they are to be men of substance, chosen from every county, so that the King can sound out the opinions of the whole country. Twenty are to be on duty at any time. They are to wear the King's livery, and to ride in attendance on him and serve at his table in the hall. The last provision goes rather beyond Jeeves's province: they must help to provide entertainment:

> These Esquires of housold be accustomed, winter and summer, in afternoones and in eueninges, to drawe to Lordes Chambres within Court, there to keep honest company after there Cunninge, in talking of Chronicles of Kinges, and of others Pollicies, or in pipeing or harpeing, songinges, or other actes marcealls, to helpe to occupie the Court, and accompanie estraingers, till the time require of departing.
>
> EDWARD IV'S HOUSEHOLD BOOK, *Chaucer Society 2nd Series*, 14. p. 70

There is a Squire among the pilgrims in the *Canterbury Tales*, travelling with the Knight, his father. He is about twenty, Chaucer's age when he was a Squire, and has served abroad in the Hundred Years' War.

With hym ther was his sone, a yong Squier,
A lovyere and a lusty bacheler,
With lokkes crulle as they were leyd in presse.   *curled*
Of twenty yeer of age he was, I gesse.
Of his stature he was of evene lengthe,
And wonderly delyvere, and of greet strengthe,   *agile*
And he hadde been somtyme in chyvachie
In Flaundres, in Artoys, and Pycardie,
And born hym weel, as of so litel space,
In hope to stonden in his lady grace.
Embrouded was he, as it were a meede   *meadow*
Al ful of fresshe floures, whyte and reede
Syngynge he was or floytynge, al the day;   *playing the flute*
He was as fresshe as is the month of May.
Short was his gowne with sleves longe and wyde.
Wel koude he sitte on hors and faire ryde.
He koude songes make and wel endite,   *compose the words*
Juste and eek daunce, and weel purtreye and write.   *draw*
So hoote he lovede that by nyghtertale
He sleep namoore than dooth a nyghtyngale.
Curteis he was, lowely, and servysable,   *humble, willing to serve*
And carf biforn his fader at the table.

CT: GEN. PROL. I, 79–100

The Court still looked towards the Continent. The English
kings held some territory in France and laid claim to still more.
French was the language of Chivalry and of civilized society.
Even if the days had passed when the King of England knew no
English, Edward III certainly used it but rarely, and his Queen,
Philippa of Hainault, was a native speaker of French. Nor must
we forget that the French King himself had spent several years as
a prisoner with Edward's Court. Moreover, further opportunities to absorb French influence came Chaucer's way in his first
few years at Court. In 1369 he was on a raid in Picardy, led by
John of Gaunt, and the following year he was 'abroad in the
King's service', probably in northern France. When we come to
examine his poetry we will find the Frenchness of his environ-
ment reflected in his work. He had also been abroad in 1368 to
some unspecified destination.

However, the next journey, in 1372–3, was perhaps the most important for his development as a poet. This was a six-month journey to Italy with two fellow commissioners to negotiate with the Doge and citizens of Genoa about the establishment of a port of entry in England for the Genoese merchants. He also visited Florence, for the King had entrusted him with some secret business in that city. Although this was a working visit demanding considerable legal ability, and not an 18th-century Grand Tour, he must have had opportunities of becoming familiar with the Italian literary scene: his own works show this clearly enough. From about this time, and certainly after his second visit six years later in 1378, we can see the influence of Italian writers as well as French. In *Troilus and Criseyde* and the *Knight's Tale*, for example, he took two poems of Boccaccio and made them his own. Petrarch also influenced him; he was still alive, but whether Chaucer ever met either of them we may never know, though it would be pleasant to think that he made his Clerk in the *Canterbury Tales* describe his own experience.

I wol yow telle a tale which that I
Lerned at Padowe of a worthy clerk. . . .

Fraunceys Petrak, the lauriat poete
Highte this clerk, whos rethorike sweet   *was called*
Enlumyned al Ytaille of poetrie. . . .   *illuminated with*
CT: CLERK'S PROL. IV, 26–33

(To put the major Italian writers into perspective, Boccaccio's dates are 1313–75, Petrarch's 1304–74, while Dante (1265–1321) had already been dead for fifty years when Chaucer visited Italy.)

The year after he had returned home from this voyage (1374) he moved from the Court at Westminster to the City of London, and on 2 June he took up the post of Controller of Customs and Subsidy of Wools, Skins and Hides in the Port of London, on condition that he wrote the accounts in his own hand, without appointing a deputy. His salary was £10 a year, with a yearly bonus of ten marks (1 mark=13s. 4d.) for good service. He also had an annuity of twenty marks from the King which continued until 1388, when he assigned his claim to another. When he took up his new post he was given an additional award from the King, of a pitcher of wine a day, and from John of Gaunt an annuity of £10. This was not his first connection with Gaunt, for his wife (Chaucer had been married for several years now to Philippa Roet, the sister of Katherine Swynford, who was to become John of Gaunt's third wife) had been in Gaunt's second wife's service for a couple of years. In 1382 he was given the additional post of Controller of the Petty Customs on wines and other goods but was allowed to appoint a permanent deputy. In 1385 he was allowed to have a deputy in the Wool Customs also, and was made Justice of the Peace and sat in Parliament as Knight of the Shire for Kent.

There was a chain of Custom Houses at the ports round the east and south coasts from Newcastle to Bristol at which Customs duties were levied on certain goods as they were exported. Wool was the most important of these, both because of the volume of trade and of the demand for it on the Continent, which made it possible for the King to increase the amount of the levy, just as today the Chancellor of the Exchequer can increase the duty on tobacco without decreasing the demand. The basic rate as established by Edward I in 1275 was 6s. 8d. on each sack of 364 lb. of wool, 6s. 8d. on each bale of 300 sheepskins, and 13s. 4d. on each last of 200 hides. This was increased in times of emergency by additional levies, which at times stood as high as 43s. 4d. on a sack of wool, making 50s. in all.

In London the House for the Wool Customs was on the Wool-wharf on the north bank of the Thames between the Tower and London Bridge. It backed on to Thames Street, where Chaucer was born. The wool was brought to the Customs House, where it was weighed in the presence of the Tronager (the official who actually did the weighing) and the Controller. The Customs were paid and the amount entered on the account rolls; when the wool was loaded the shipmaster came to swear that he had paid all duties on his cargo, and he was given a receipt.

All this time Chaucer had been living in a house over Aldgate which he had leased from the Mayor and Aldermen of London in the summer of 1374. Aldgate was the eastern-most gate in the city walls, and it commanded the road out to Mile End and thence to Essex. Here a good deal of his poetry was written. This was the 'house' mentioned by the eagle in the *House of Fame*, who had instructions to liven the old stick-in-the-mud up a bit:

> . . . For when thy labour doon al ys,
> And hast mad alle thy rekenynges,
> In stede of rest and newe thynges,
> Thou goost hom to thy hous anoon;
> And, also domb as any stoon,   *as dumb as*
> Thou sittest at another book
> Tyl fully daswed ys thy look. . . .   *dazed*
>
> HOUSE OF FAME 652–8

In 1386 his luck seems to have turned: he lost his official positions and his house. John of Gaunt, his protector, had left the country in July, and the young King Richard II had to face increasing hostility from his Court. A purge followed, in which several great lords lost their positions and, amongst the lesser officials, Nicholas Brembre, several times Lord Mayor of London and a collector of Customs under Chaucer, lost his life. So it may well be that Chaucer's departure from official life was forced upon him. The following year his wife died. Thus he was left with nothing to occupy him but his poetry, and it is in this period that he began to collect together the *Canterbury Tales*.

Three years later the tables turned once more; Richard declared himself to be of full age and took upon himself his full rights as King. In July 1389, two months after he had assumed his powers, he appointed Chaucer to the very important post of Clerk of the King's Works, which William of Wykeham, the Chancellor of England and founder of Winchester College and New College, Oxford, had held before him. This meant that he was in charge of the fabric of the Tower of London, Westminster Palace and eight other royal manors. At all of these he was responsible for all building and repair work. The following year he had the additional duty of attending to repairs to St. George's Chapel, Windsor. (Not the present splendid St. George's Chapel, which dates from the reign of Henry V, but its predecessor.) He had also been appointed to inspect the walls, bridges, sewers, gutters, ditches, roads and ponds along the Thames between Greenwich and Woolwich, to assess the responsibility for their decay and to compel the owners of adjoining properties to make repairs. After two years as Clerk of Works Chaucer resigned, and took up the sinecure of the subforestership of the Forest of North Petherton in Somerset. He had been robbed and beaten up twice as he went about his duties, and, what is more, the King owed him a considerable sum of money when he resigned from the Clerkship. There is no wonder that he should go into retirement, for he was fifty now and expectation of life was far less in those days. Nevertheless he lived on for several years. In December 1399 he took a fifty-three-year lease, rather optimistically perhaps, of a house in the garden of Westminster Abbey: he lived in it for less than a year, and died on 25 October 1400. He is buried in the Abbey in the spot that was later to become known as the 'Poets' Corner'.

2

Social Life

So much for a brief outline of the main events of Chaucer's life.
He was an important and cultured person living in close contact
with the Court, the seat of power. Although we can assume that
he is not unlike the audience of his contemporaries for whom he
wrote his poems, we cannot use his life to show what the lives
of the bulk of the population were like. Chaucer was one of the
favoured few, writing for the favoured few. But he also portrayed representatives of almost the whole of society in his
Canterbury Tales. We ought now to try to sketch in their role in
society, especially since society was so differently constituted then.

THE LAND

In the first half of the 14th century about ninety per cent of the
total population of four and a half million lived on the land,
mainly in scattered villages each holding some 50 to 200 people.
The land itself belonged to the Lord of the Manor and was split
up, not into individual holdings, but into communal fields
farmed on the strip system; there was also the Lord's demesne, or
home farm, which was worked by the villagers in lieu of rent for
their own strips. Not all the villagers were equal: there was a
fundamental division between freeman and serf (or villein).
Freemen were the Lord's tenants; the serfs were his property:
they were bound to the soil and could, at least theoretically, be
bought and sold like cattle.

A village was, on the whole, self-sufficient. The fields produced
enough food; the sheep provided raw material for clothing; the
surrounding waste land gave firewood and building materials.
There was a mill for grinding the corn, and a church and a priest

to look after spiritual needs. The organization of village life fell chiefly upon the reeve. He was the villagers' elected representative; his duties involved him in the day-to-day running of the manor by organizing the work on the Lord's demesne, seeing that all who were liable contributed the proper number of days of labour without shirking. He had to guard against pilfering, ensure that the livestock was properly cared for, and look after the tools, equipment and farm buildings. If the manor made a profit he had to produce it at the end of the year, and if there was a loss he was personally responsible for making up the deficit. With these opportunities for squeezing the last ounce out of the villagers and diverting it to his own pocket, it is not surprising that some reeves made the most of them and became oppressors rather than representatives. On the owner's side, supervision was often delegated to a bailiff or steward (depending on the importance of the landlord). Together with the reeve he had to submit the accounts to a most stringent auditing.

The *Prologue* shows a reeve who clearly took advantage of all his opportunities for squeezing the villeins at the same time as cheating the Lord of the Manor:

Wel koude he kepe a gerner and a bynne;	*granary*
Ther was noon auditour koude on him wynne.	*get the better of*
Wel wiste he by the droghte and by the reyn	
The yeldynge of his seed and of his greyn.	*yield*
His lordes sheep, his neet, his dayerye,	*cattle*
His swyn, his hors, his stoor, and his pultrye	*stock*
Was hooly in this Reves governynge,	
And by his covenant yaf the rekenynge,	*presented the accounts*
Syn that his lord was twenty yeer of age.	
Ther koude no man brynge hym in arrerage.	*arrears*
Ther nas baillif, ne hierde, nor oother hyne,	*herdsman labourer*
That he ne knew his sleighte and his covyne;	*trickery deceit*
They were adrad of hym as of the deeth.	*afraid*
His wonyng was ful faire upon an heeth;	*house*
With grene trees yshadwed was his place.	
He koude bettre than his lord purchace.	
Ful riche he was astored pryvely:	*secretly*
His lord wel koude he plesen subtilly,	

To yeve and lene hym of his owene good,   *lend   possessions*
And have a thank and yet a cote and hood.

CT: GEN. PROL. I, 593–612

The *Reeve's Tale*, about how a dishonest miller was outwitted
by a couple of Cambridge students, shows that reeves were not
alone in being able to line their pockets at others' expense. We
must, of course, make allowance for the feud between Chaucer's
Miller and his Reeve; neither is likely to speak well of the other.
Yet the Miller on the pilgrimage is not as honest as he might be:

> Wel koude he stelen corn and tollen thries.

His main opportunity arose because the mill belonged to the
Lord of the Manor who compelled all his tenants to take their
corn to be ground there: if they were dissatisfied, they had to
put up with it; they could not take their business elsewhere.

Throughout the 14th century there was a gradual change in
the organization of rural society in the direction of money, wages
and rent, and away from the old villeinage and labour dues. By
the end of the century it no longer paid the Lord of the Manor to
farm his demesne for himself. It was more efficient to rent land
out and pay wages to the labourers who then were working more
willingly. In fact, many landlords no longer lived on the manor at
all, and a new class of almost 'gentleman farmer' sprang up. Such
a one is the Franklin: he certainly had plenty of money if the
way it snowed food and drink in his house is anything to go by;
he was travelling with the Sergeant of the Law, who was both
rich and important. The Franklin was in fact the equivalent of
the country squire of later times on whom much of the smooth
running of the countryside with the administration of justice and
other duties depended. He is a 14th-century Squire Western.

> At sessiouns ther was he lord and sire;
> Ful ofte tyme he was knyght of the shire.
> An anlaas and a gipser al of silk   *dagger   purse*
> Heeng at his girdel, whit as morne milk.
> A shirreve hadde he been, and a contour.   *sheriff   auditor*
> Was nowher swich a worthy vavasour.   *land-holder*

CT: GEN. PROL. I, 355–60

The social change of which the Franklin is one symptom was accelerated by the advent of the Black Death. By the middle of the century the old agricultural economy was at its highest point. During the 300 years since the Norman Conquest, the population had trebled in number to something around four and a half million. Land was scarce and labour plentiful; the landlords held the whip hand. But in 1348–9 the bubonic plague struck for the first time for centuries. Over the country as a whole perhaps one-third of the population lost their lives, but obviously in some places a far greater proportion than this died: in Witney, for instance, the mortality rate was sixty per cent, but some villages were wiped out entirely. Nor was this the only visitation: the plague re-appeared in 1361, 1363, 1375, and every ten to fifteen years thereafter until the Great Plague of London in 1665 (which was in actual fact no greater than its predecessors—it merely had a Defoe to chronicle it). In these years the mortality rate was from three to six times the normal, and this imposed a tremendous long-term strain on the economy.

The decline in the population led to a social revolution. Land was no longer scarce, so its value fell, bringing down the income of the most wealthy. But also labour was now at a premium; the labourer found himself in demand, and could dictate his terms, thus hastening the change-over from compelled villein to voluntarily hired labourer. The gap between rich and poor was thus reduced considerably. The rich did not like the new situation, and in 1351 came the Statute of Labourers, which sought to curb wages by legislation. This failed, as it was bound to do—there is always someone ready to pay over the odds to poach scarce labour. But the situation remained tense until the Peasants' Revolt of 1381, the first violent social revolution in English history. It was sparked off by the heavy poll tax of 1381, which was imposed on rich and poor alike to pay for the Hundred Years' War. All over the south and east the peasants took to arms, and two well-disciplined bands converged on London from Kent and Essex. On 13 June they entered the city, besieged the Court in the Tower of London, captured and killed the Archbishop of Canterbury and destroyed several of the town houses of the local landowners, among them the Savoy which belonged to John of Gaunt; he fortunately had taken the precaution of crossing the border to Scotland. The next day, the 14th, Richard II, then only a boy of fourteen, rode out to Mile End to meet the rebels and conceded the end of villeinage. There followed a second meeting the day after, this time at Smithfield, where the leader of the Kentish band, Wat Tyler, presented more demands. These, too, were granted, whereupon the Lord Mayor of London, William Walworth, pulled Tyler from his horse and slew him with his sword. Strange as it may seem, the royal party were not harmed. The young King appealed to the rebels to take him as their leader: 'Sirs, will you shoot your King? I am your captain, follow me'. And follow him they did, obeying his instructions to disperse in peace.

No sooner was the situation eased than the ruling classes firmly reasserted themselves. The concessions were all withdrawn and outbreaks of revolt up and down the country were put down with force. The King's reply to a deputation from Essex demanding ratification of the promises given at Mile End was blunt and to the point: 'Villeins ye are and villeins ye shall remain'. Thus the last sparks of resistance in Essex were crushed at Billericay. The pattern was the same everywhere. All the revolt had done was to put back the emancipation of the peasant by several years, but yet it had to come. The changing economic scene ensured that.

THE TOWNS: LONDON

Whereas the bulk of the population lived in the country and perhaps fifty per cent of those were villeins, only ten per cent, less than half a million, all of them free, lived in the towns. London was of course the largest, with a population of 35,000–40,000 in the mid-14th century; and York came a long way second with 11,000, Bristol third with 10,000, then Plymouth and Coventry with 7,000. As a comparison, contemporary Florence had 90,000; and modern York has 110,000. After the Norman Conquest, Winchester lost place to London as the capital of the country, while the Court, the centre of government, was establishing itself two miles upstream from the City at Westminster. Between the two was a stretch of open country with a road along the banks of the Thames, the Strand, which was lined with the town houses of the greater nobles. John of Gaunt's at the Savoy, the one sacked during the Peasants' Revolt, was 'a house more beautiful than any other in the kingdom'. London itself was confined to the square mile within the city walls.

> Upstream to the west, the Royal Palace towers above the river. It is a building without equal, with outworks and bastions, two miles from the city, and joined to it by a crowded suburb. On both sides, the beautiful and spacious tree-planted gardens of the citizens, who dwell in the suburbs, lie close together.
>
> LIFE OF ST. THOMAS, William Fitzstephen, Prol. 5–6

This description was written two centuries before, in the last quarter of the 12th century, but it is borne out by an 18th-century re-engraving of a map showing London as it was in 1563. On it there is no more than ribbon development along Fleet Street and the Strand; Covent Garden really was a garden, and Oxford Road is a country lane running between fields on its way to Oxford. The Thames was crossed by the old London Bridge, completed in 1209, and not replaced until 1831. It had many narrow arches and carried on top a row of houses like the Ponte Vecchio at Florence, as can be seen from the background of a late 15th-century view of the Tower of London in a manuscript in the British Museum (see the illustration after p. 72). At its farther end, on the south bank of the Thames, lay the suburb of Southwark where a Harry Bailey (the innkeeper of the *Canterbury Tales*) actually kept an inn in the 1370's and 1380's.

It was in these surroundings that Chaucer grew up. His father, John Chaucer, was a wine merchant and a member of the Vintners' Company, who owned a house in Thames Street, which still runs parallel to the river from the Tower of London to Blackfriars Bridge, though then it ran along the river wall. It was quite a select area, though the Walbrook, which formed one boundary of his property, was at times virtually an open sewer. The district was the headquarters of the wine trade; the same parish, that of St. Martin at Vintry, also held the Vintners' Hall (the present building dates only from 1671). The wine trade, like all other trades, was controlled by a central organization. Collectively these Companies or Guilds of Merchants (or other trades such as the Masons and Barbers) were the most important organizations in the life of the City, for only men who were full members of a guild were admitted to the full rights, privileges and duties of citizenship. On their shoulders fell the government of the City, and they had to bear their share of taxation and public duties: from among them were elected the Aldermen who formed the City Council (and still do). But on the other hand they were the only people with political rights, and furthermore only they could legally engage in retail trade. So, though Chaucer does not give a detailed description of those five of his pilgrims who were tradesmen, we should not dismiss them as mere small shopkeepers—their wives knew better than this!

An Haberdasshere and a Carpenter,		
A Webbe, a Dyere, and a Tapycer,—	*weaver*	*tapestry-weaver*
And they were clothed alle in o lyveree		*one*
Of a solempne and a greet fraternitee.		
Ful fressh and newe hir geere apiked was;	*apparel*	*trimmed*
Hir knyes were chaped noght with bras		*mounted*
But al with silver; wroght ful clene and weel		
Hire girdles and hir pouches everydeel.		
Wel semed ech of hem a fair burgeys		*burgess*
To sitten in a yeldehalle on a deys.		*guildhall*
Everich, for the wisdom that he kan,		
Was shaply for to been an alderman.		*fitted*
For catel hadde they ynogh and rente,		*property*
And eek hir wyves wolde it wel assente;		
And elles certeyn were they to blame.		
It is ful fair to been ycleped 'madame',		*called*
And goon to vigilies al bifore,		*before everyone*
And have a mantel roialliche ybore.		

CT: GEN. PROL. I, 361–78

The great variety of trades could not, of course, be represented in one guild; as line 364 suggests, cutting across the trade guild structure was another sort of society, the fraternity, whose objects were social and religious, much like the Rotary International today.

Not all who lived in London could be citizens; there was a considerable number of outsiders, both native and foreigners (though naturally the English predominated). These, in theory, could not make their living by the retail trade, but had to content themselves with the lower jobs, as casual labourers, porters and the like, or by manufacturing goods for sale by the true citizens. There was also a fluctuating population whose business was with the Court: officials who could not be housed in Westminster; hangers-on at Court; and those who had been brought there by the law, either as litigants, lawyers or students. The lawyers and students were catered for largely by the Inns of Court, which were not actually in the City itself but to the west, just off the Strand, where they are still. The Inner Temple, at least, was already in existence, and provided not merely training in the law as it does today, but a complete education in itself, rivalling that given by the Universities of Oxford and Cambridge. It had the advantage of being completely secular, and attracted the sons of the nobility and landed gentry. Chaucer pokes fun at the inhabitants of a Temple through his Manciple, the official responsible for buying the provisions (All Souls College, Oxford, still has an official with the title of Manciple):

Of maistres hadde he mo than thries ten,	*masters*
That were of lawe expert and curious,	*skilled*
Of which ther were a duszeyne in that hous	
Worthy to been stywardes of rente and lond	
Of any lord that is in Engelond,	
To make hym lyve by his propre good,	*on his own income*
In honour dettelees (but if he were wood),	*unless mad*
Or lyve as scarsly as hym list desire;	*thriftily*
And able for to helpen al a shire	
In any caas that myghte falle or happe;	*disaster*
And yet this Manciple sette hir aller cappe.	*got the better of*
	all of them

CT: GEN. PROL. I, 567–86

It is amusing that before Chaucer tells us about the tricky Manciple he has already described in fulsome terms one of the high dignitaries of the law who might well have been one of the *maistres* in the first line above (line 576). There were in fact only twenty Sergeants in Chaucer's time, so this one must have been a really important man, truly 'full riche of excellence' . . .

So greet a purchasour was nowher noon:	*land buyer*
Al was fee symple to hym in effect;	*unrestricted possession*
His purchasyng myghte nat been infect.	*set aside*
Nowher so bisy a man as he ther nas,	
And yet he semed bisier than he was.	
In termes hadde he caas and doomes alle	*accurately cases judgements*
That from the tyme of kyng William were falle.	
Therto he koude endite, and make a thyng,	*write*
Ther koude no wight pynche at his writyng;	*so that complain*
And every statut koude he pleyn by rote.	*say by heart*

CT: GEN. PROL. I, 318–27

Chaucer makes it very clear that his dignified and perhaps pompous professional lawyer was on the make.

THE CHURCH

The two universities, on the other hand, were under the control of the Church, and this highlights another important distinction of medieval society, that between the layman and the cleric. There were in fact two entirely different orders of society. All clerics had been set apart from their fellow men and had received certain privileges and obligations; but this does not make them into a uniform class, and we should not imagine that a medieval cleric, or clerk, is the same as a modern clergyman. What the clergy had in common was the 'first tonsure' or symbolic shaving of the head, the oath of celibacy and the privileges of clerical dress and 'Benefit of Clergy', which bestowed the right to be tried for all offences by the clerical courts which existed side by side with the secular ones, but which were far more lenient and gave comparative immunity to first offenders. The Summoner of such a court was part of the ecclesiastical machinery of justice;

his job, as his title suggests, was to summon the malefactors to appear before the ecclesiastical court, which was usually presided over by the local Archdeacon. Chaucer's Summoner quotes the opening of one of the writs he sometimes carried, that remanding an excommunicated person to prison: *Significavit nobis venerabilis pater*—but this must have been one of his rarer jobs. Our man is not a particularly nice specimen, but according to the Friar (not an unbiased witness!) the Summoner was not at all atypical, for:

> Pardee, ye may wel knowe by the name
> That of a somonour may no good be sayd;
> I preye that noon of you be yvele apayd.   *suffer*
> A somonour is a rennere up and doun   *runner*
> With mandementz for fornicacioun,   *summonses*
> And is ybet at every townes ende.   *beaten*
>
> CT: FRIAR'S PROL. III, 1280–5

The tonsure was only the first step in a career in the Church. Many went no further, and had no need to. Up to the 13th century, all educated men belonged to the clerical classes; this meant that most lawyers and doctors (medicine was certainly taught at Oxford in the 14th century—John of Gaddesden, one of the authorities mentioned in the description of the Doctor of Physic in the *Prologue*, taught at Merton College), all scholars, students and graduates of the universities, and even most grammar school boys had taken the tonsure. In fact, in the 13th century one in fifty of the whole population was a cleric. But because the professions and civil service were staffed by clerics, many had no need to go farther in the Church—at least until they retired to a living or a bishopric, and then they would pass through the necessary stages of Holy Orders—sub-deacon, deacon, priest—as quickly as possible. Before the need arose they saw no point in burdening themselves with clerical responsibility.

In Chaucer's time the situation was changing. Laymen could now qualify for the civil service since, as we have seen, the Inns of Court provided a first-class secular education: Chaucer himself is sufficient proof that laymen could find employment at Court.

We may quite easily forget that when we talk of the Church in Chaucer's time we mean the Roman Catholic Church, for at this date the only Christian Church that had a separate existence from it was the Greek Orthodox Church; the Reformation, from which sprang the Protestant Churches, was yet to come, though the first stirrings might just be audible. We have therefore to allow for this great difference: there was in England (and in Western Europe) only one Church.

Beside the *secular* clergy who carried out the functions of the modern clergyman there were the *regular* clergy who had taken the vows of communal life, and whose function was prayer and meditation rather than the cure of souls. Furthermore, the church services were conducted in Latin and the chief of these was the Mass. The organization of the secular clergy was much as it is today, though boundaries have changed and new dioceses have been created. The basis was the parish covering a village, or a group of hamlets, or a few streets in a town, and containing perhaps 400 people; these were grouped into archdeaconries covering roughly the area of a modern county, and these in turn were arranged in dioceses under a bishop. Unfortunately, not all of the secular clergy were like Chaucer's Parson; many had not the training or the ability—or, indeed, the conscientiousness—to look after their flocks as well as he did. Many priests were recruited from the peasant class and so were of servile origin; Chaucer's Parson, whose brother was a ploughman, managed to overcome any such handicap and set a fine example to his people. Indeed, it was not unknown for others to rise from such humble beginnings to the highest posts in Church and State. But it must be admitted that such men are few; the records of the ecclesiastical courts and the bishop's visitations, in which he took stock of each of the parishes in his diocese in turn, make sorry reading, for the parish clergy were often not up to their jobs.

The other major abuse was absenteeism. Each parish drew revenue from its glebe land, which belonged to the Church, and also from tithes levied upon the parishioners' produce. This made a benefice a desirable piece of property, especially when the incumbent, or rector, was able to instal a vicar (a word which means a substitute) to carry out the duties, and to pay him a stipend less than the revenue. Thus originally a vicar had a far lower position than a rector: the two were not equals, as they are today. Some of these absentee priests might have a good reason for not residing in their parishes: one might be a scholar at the university and get his living from his benefice. But many left because they could find themselves a more profitable position elsewhere, as chaplains to a Guild or Fraternity or at a Chantry where Masses were said for the soul of the founder. By contrast to this, Chaucer's Parson stands out, as he is intended to do, as an example of a model parish priest:

> . . . But riche he was of hooly thoght and werk.
> He was also a lerned man, a clerk,
> That Cristes gospel trewely wolde preche . . .   *[excommunicate*
>
> Ful looth were hym to cursen for his tithes,   *he was unwilling to*
> But rather wolde he yeven, out of doute,   *give*
> Unto his povre parisshens aboute
> Of his offryng and eek of his substaunce . . .
> He sette nat his benefice to hyre   *hire out*
> And leet his sheep encombred in the myre   *left*
> And ran to Londoun unto Seinte Poules
> To seken hym a chaunterie for soules,   *chantry*
> Or with a bretherhed to been withholde;   *kept apart*
> But dwelte at hoom, and kepte wel his folde,
> So that the wolf ne made it nat myscarie;
> He was a shepherde and noght a mercenarie . . .
>
> . . . But Cristes loore and his apostles twelve
> He taughte, but first he folwed it hymselve.

CT: GEN. PROL. I, 479–528

It is clear that Chaucer idealized this Parson of a Toun just as much as he did the Knight; both of them laboured faithfully in their vocation, and were certainly unusual in their selflessness.

THE RELIGIOUS LIFE

The vocation of the *secular* clergy, such as the Parson, was to minister to the daily needs of their parishioners. The *regular* clergy (so called because they were bound by a rule of life—Latin: *regula*) were not involved with the life of the world—in theory, that is. Their vocation was to a life of prayer, meditation and study, called the religious life, the *vita contemplativa*, as opposed to the *vita activa*. It was open to women as well as to men, and those who followed it lived a communal life apart as monks and nuns. When Criseyde in *Troilus and Criseyde* says she is 'not religious', she means not that she does not believe in God, but that she is not a nun, bound to the religious life; for that is what the term 'religious' implies.

The communal religious life was the invention of St. Benedict who founded the first monastery in Italy in 529. The Benedictine Rule which he laid down was for many years the model for these communities. It was austere, intended to train its followers for positions in the forefront of religious and intellectual life: and for a considerable time this purpose was indeed fulfilled. From the 10th century onwards, other orders of monks branched out, each with its own modified rule varying mainly in strictness and the proportion of manual labour to intellectual. Every man who entered a monastery, of whatever order, renounced by doing so all personal possessions, and bound himself to a communal life of poverty with a fixed routine of prayer, meditation, liturgy (church service ritual), work and even diet. But over the centuries things tended to become slack: even if individuals could not own property the community could, and most of them amassed vast estates, which tended to increase the slackness: it becomes harder to practise poverty where wealth is available. In fact, many monks must have become more like country gentlemen. It is well known, however, that scandalous behaviour attracts more attention than ordinary sober life. Even if the monasteries and convents were no longer, in Chaucer's time, the homes of devout intellectuals, they were more likely to be run with a stable respectability than to be given over entirely to the affairs of this world, as Chaucer's portraits of the Monk and the Prioress might lead us to suppose. The Prioress shows one form of lapse: from simplicity to sophistication; she may have been the head of a convent of nuns, but she would not have been out of place at Court. Her affected French, her exquisite table manners, her tender-hearted concern for her overfed pet dogs (contrasting most sharply with the Parson's concern for his poor parishioners) and her fashionable clothes and coiffure are all evidence of a worldly nature, and in the end one is tempted to wonder whether the Love which her brooch proclaimed was not perhaps more secular than it ought to be.

> Of smal coral aboute hire arm she bar
> A peire of bedes, gauded al with grene,   *rosary   decorated*
> And theron heng a brooch of gold ful sheene,   *shining*
> On which ther was first write a crowned A
> And after *Amor vincit omnia.*   *Love conquers all*
>
> CT: GEN. PROL. I, 158–62

A similar conjecture cannot be avoided in the case of the Monk, 'a manly man to been an abbot able', who wore 'a ful curious pin' of gold, in the 'gretter ende' of which there was a love-knot. Chaucer leaves us in no doubt, however, about his hunting, his rejection of study and meditation, and his love of a fat swan for dinner.

> . . . The reule of seint Maure or of Seint Beneit,
> By cause that it was old and somdel streit   *strict*
> This ilke Monk leet olde thynges pace,   *pass*
> And heeld after the newe world the space.
> He yaf nat of that text a pulled hen,
> That seith that hunters ben nat hooly men,
> Ne that a monk, whan he is recchelees,   *forgetful of his duty*
> Is likned til a fissh that is waterlees,—
> This is to seyn, a monk out of his cloystre. . . .
>
> What sholde he studie and make hymselven wood,   *mad*
> Upon a book in cloystre alwey to poure,
> Or swynken with his handes, and laboure,   *toil*
> As Austyn bit? How shal the world be served?   *Augustine ordained*
> Let Austyn have his swynk to hym reserved!   *labour*
>
> CT: GEN. PROL. I, 172–88

Such an attitude to the *vita contemplativa* could not have been universal, but it was obviously common enough to merit Chaucer's censure.

So much for Chaucer's picture of regular and secular clergy, though it must be pointed out that their functions were in fact less separate and distinct than has been made out; for the regular clergy could and did become priests, and the bishops of some dioceses were monks, their cathedrals being monasteries at the same time—as the cloisters in Salisbury Cathedral, for instance, still witness. In the first quarter of the 13th century, however, rivals appeared on the scene. These were the four Orders of Friars, which included the Franciscans, founded by St. Francis of Assisi (1181–1226), and known as the Grey Friars from the colour of their dress; and the Dominicans, or Black Friars, founded by St. Dominic (1170–1221). Their originators had intended them to set an example of apostolic poverty such as Jesus enjoined on his disciples; they were to reject corporate as well as personal property. And St. Dominic also directed the energies of his followers towards preaching. Unlike the regular Orders, the Friars were not confined to the cloister; in fact, they had to make their way through the world begging their living as they went— hence their title of Mendicants. They formed a third force who could exercise all the functions of the parish priests without the supervision of the bishops, who had no control over them at all. This naturally did not make them popular with the secular clergy, but they were in great demand with the laymen from whom they begged their living. Their strongest point, however, was their scholarship: they revitalized the universities with their devotion to learning: but this is the last thing one would guess from the description of the Friar in the *Canterbury Tales*! He is another example of the corruption of an ideal. Friars had begun to live together in companies even though they still had to beg, and Chaucer's Friar was 'the beste beggere in his hous'. In fact, this was his job: he was a *limitour*, which means that he had the exclusive right to beg in a certain area, within prescribed limits. At the same time he heard confessions, and was more lenient than the parish clergy, as well he might be, since his living depended directly on his clemency. As Chaucer says:

Cc

Ful wel biloved and famulier was he
With frankeleyns over al in his contree,   *more than any other*
And eek with worthy wommen of the toun;
For he hadde power of confessioun,
As seyde hymself, moore than a curat,
For of his ordre he was licenciat.   *licensed to hear confessions*
Ful swetely herde he confessioun,
And plesaunt was his absolucioun:
He was an esy man to yeve penaunce,
Ther as he wiste to have a good pitaunce,   *offering*
For unto a povre ordre for to yive
Is signe that a man is well yshryve. . . .   *has made a good confession*

Begging was not his sole accomplishment, though, for:

. . . certeinly he hadde a murye note:
Wel koude he synge and pleyen on a rote;   *small harp*
Of yeddynges he bar outrely the pris . . .   *songs   absolutely*
. . . And in his harpyng, whan that he hadde songe,
His eyen twynkled in his heed aryght,
As doon the sterres in the frosty nyght.

CT: GEN. PROL. I, 215-68

But of all the clerics in the *Canterbury Tales*, perhaps the Pardoner is the one who meets with the least sympathy today.
(Most pardoners were in minor orders, though some were laymen.) The Summoner has a useful job to do, even if he takes the
opportunity to make a bit on the side. But nowadays few people
in this country believe in indulgences, which were the Pardoner's
stock-in-trade. The theory of indulgences is based on the Catholic
teaching that the merits of the saints can be credited to the
account, as it were, of other deserving members of the Church.
Saints lay up a stock of merit for ordinary folk to draw on. It
was common practice to reward those who had contributed to
the building or upkeep of Church property with an indulgence
written on parchment with the Papal seal attached; this would
reduce penance in this world and mitigate the pains of Purgatory
in the next. As a practice it was clearly open to abuse: the activities of the pardoners who hawked the Papal indulgences granted
to those who had contributed to the completion of St. Peter's in

Rome were one of the sparks that set off the Reformation, for it was very easy to appear to be *selling* the indulgences rather than to be rewarding pious contributors with them, and we may be sure that not all contributions made their way to the relevant building fund, whether that of St. Peter's, or somewhere more local, like that of the Hospital of the Blessed Mary of Rouncivalle, just outside London at Charing Cross, to which Chaucer's Pardoner was attached. He had come straight from Rome:

> His walet lay biforn hym in his lappe,
> Bretful of pardoun, comen from Rome al hoot. . . .   *chock full*

> . . . of his craft, from Berwyk unto Ware,
> Ne was ther swich another pardoner
> For in his male he hadde a pilwe-beer,   *bag pillow-case*
> Which that he seyde was Oure Lady veyl:
> He seyde he hadde a gobet of the seyl   *piece*
> That Seint Peter hadde, whan that he wente
> Upon the see, til Jhesu Crist hym hente.   *chose*
> He hadde a croys of latoun ful of stones,   *cross copper alloy*
> And in a glas he hadde pigges bones.
> But with thise relikes, whan that he fond
> A povre person dwellynge upon lond,   *parson in the country*
> Upon a day he gat hym moore moneye
> Than that the person gat in monthes tweye;
> And thus, with feyned flaterye and japes,   *tricks*
> He made the person and the peple his apes.   *dupes*
> CT: GEN. PROL. I, 686–706

It is his second line of business, the selling of the false relics of saints, that we find more distasteful. Perhaps if more clergy had been like the Parson, or the Clerk of Oxford who was still in training, there would have been fewer pardoners to get an easy living from the credulity of the ignorant; but rogues inhabit every age. The Pardoner and his like were helped by the vast contrasts we find in the Middle Ages between the top and the bottom of society, between the ideal and the realization, not only in secular life but in the Church also.

3

Science

In this chapter I want to sketch in the background of thought, before which people of the 14th century lived their lives. Just as we all share a common stock of ideas—scientific, moral, philosophical—though we may not have them very clear in our minds and could not give adequate expression to them, so in Chaucer's day everybody took for granted certain basic assumptions about human nature, the influence of the stars, the constitution of matter and the right way to live their lives. For instance, if today we read in the newspapers that the jet record to Australia has been smashed, we can all conceive an image of a particular sort of aeroplane (though we may not know much of how the engine actually works, and nothing at all of aerodynamics), and a picture of a round world on the other side of which, 12,000 miles away, is a land-mass of a particular shape and with a particular sort of climate and way of life. Again, we all know what sort of activity is implied in 'smashing a record', and we can all feel something of the excitement of the aeronauts and designers, because we all share the same competitive spirit that has been inculcated into us as part of the modern philosophy of life (though we might secretly, or even openly, despise its main manifestation, which we may allude to as 'the rat-race').

So with Chaucer's readers. He didn't need to explain to them what the *First Mover* was, or the effect of the *humours*: but we have to have these things explained if we are to enjoy his poetry to the full as readers in his own day did.

First, then, let us look at Chaucer's physical world, so different from ours as we see it today. We live in an expanding universe. Our planet is one of nine, circling an insignificant star on the edge of a disc-shaped galaxy, which we call the Milky Way. This galaxy is one of an almost countless number: certainly thousands of millions of others, which astronomers have observed. They are all receding from us and from each other at speeds which increase with distance, so that the most distant ones are travelling away from us almost with the speed of light. This, in a few words, is one picture, or model of the universe which seems to fit the observations of modern astronomers, and it was such terms as these that Professor Lovell used in his Reith Lectures (1962) to explain the modern view of astronomy to the general public. The distances involved are so vast that even to us moderns they are almost meaningless; the light from the nearest star takes four years to reach us, travelling at 186,325 miles a second, and that from the farthest galaxies takes centuries. It may be just as well that in our cities the street lights outshine the stars, for it can be a frightening experience to gaze up at the night sky and try to imagine what is meant by infinity. In his auto-biography Arthur Koestler tells how at the age of thirteen he lay back on a hillside near Budapest and thought about infinity:

> You could shoot a super-arrow into the blue with a super-force which would carry it beyond the pull of the Earth's gravity, past the moon, past the sun's attraction—and what then? It would traverse interstellar space, pass other suns, other galaxies, Milky Ways, Honeyed Ways, Acid Ways—and what then? It would go on and on, past the spiral nebulae, and more galaxies and more spiral nebulae, and there would be nothing to stop it, no limit and no end, in space or time.

ARROW IN THE BLUE 51

The medieval view of the universe, which was believed in from classical times until the scientific revolution of the 17th century, when the foundations of modern science were laid, was quite different. It was finite in size and, though not as small as some modern writers have patronizingly supposed, it was not so big that, like ours, it became incomprehensible.

When Chaucer looked out from his bedroom window at night, though he saw the same objects in the heavens as Koestler did, he had quite a different conception of their organization. He stood on a solid ball of Earth, which did not move at all; he saw the various planets, seven of them (he had no telescope), move at different speeds across the sky, and he saw the main body of stars, fixed in the same relative position to each other, move round the Earth in a regular and ordered manner. To account for the fact that the planets—he thought they were the Moon, Mercury, Venus, Sun, Mars, Jupiter and Saturn, in that order of distance from him—moved at different speeds and in varying paths, he saw them as separately fixed on seven concentric transparent spheres of crystal arranged like the layers of an onion in the centre of which he stood. Outside these seven continually revolving spheres was an eighth, on which all the other stars were fixed immovably: the *Stellatum*, to give it its Latin name. Outside this again was yet another sphere, the ninth, called the *Primum Mobile*, or the First Mover: it was invisible, yet it imparted its motion to the other eight which revolved inside it at varying speeds. It was the outer boundary of the created universe: beyond it was heaven itself, the realm of God. This can lead to confusion because in ancient literature each sphere can also be referred to as a heaven—hence the old expression, 'the seventh heaven'.

There were several conflicting estimates of the size of this universe, which is not altogether surprising because medieval writers had little interest in accurate comparisons of size. (And not only writers: the same is even more true in art. Until the Renaissance, artists used only a very rudimentary form of perspective, though Dante, in the *Paradiso*, explains how objects appear smaller as they become more distant from the observer.) But if we try to extract dimensions from these scattered references —and it would not be easy—we are guilty of reading literature as if it were a scientific treatise. One account, dating from a century before the *Canterbury Tales*, says that if a man were to travel upwards at a speed of forty miles a day and more, it would take him over 8,000 years to reach the *Stellatum*; in fact if Adam had started off when he was first created he would still have a thousand years to go. A quick piece of arithmetic makes the distance well over 100,000,000 miles. But such a literal reading is a wrong use of the passage, which is taken from the *South English Legendary*, a collection of popular stories about the saints intended to instruct and entertain the common people. The greatness of the distance is important for the story; the actual figures quite irrelevant. Other passages from more learned writers are harder to misread in this way, for their purpose is to point a moral by showing how insignificant this world is in relation to the rest of the universe, and though a guided tour of the heavens is usually thrown in, it is the *moral* and not the *mechanics* of the story that matter to the writer.

The prototype of these tours is in Latin. It comes from the *Somnium Scipionis*, or *Dream of Scipio*, in Cicero's *Republic*. Because Chaucer used it more than once and because it introduces another aspect of his universe, we turn to it next. In it the younger Scipio dreams that his grandfather, Scipio Africanus, carries him up to a high place filled with stars, the *Stellatum*, from which he can see that:

> There were stars that we never see from the earth, and all of them much bigger than we have ever imagined. . . . The stars easily surpassed the earth in size; the earth itself appeared so tiny to me that I was ashamed of our empire (i.e. the Roman Empire), which covers no more than a single point, as it were, of its surface.
>
> REPUBLIC, Cicero, Book VI, 16

Chaucer knew the *Dream*. He could hardly fail to, for this ascent into the heavens became a commonplace of medieval literature. He used it in the introduction to his *Parlement of Foules*:

> . . . And after shewede he hym the nyne speres,   *spheres*
> And after that the melodye herde he
> That cometh of thilke speres thryes thre,
> That welle is of musik and melodye   *source*
> In this world here, and cause of armonye.
>
> PARLEMENT OF FOULES 59–63

Cicero explains more fully. Each sphere, animated by a divine Intelligence, emits a musical note as it spins, as if it were a humming top. Because the distance between them, and the speeds at which they spin, vary, they produce different notes. Thus

39

between them they cover a whole octave. This heavenly octave is usually known as the music of the spheres, and is the pattern of all earthly music. Unfortunately, despite Milton's invocation— 'Ring out, ye crystal spheres'—we cannot hear it. Our bodies are too gross and earthy, and, having been exposed to it incessantly since our birth, we are no more aware of it than people who live within earshot of a waterfall are aware of the roar of water

The doctrine of the music of the spheres has a long history. It was propounded by Pythagoras and his followers (who, incidentally, had no complete proof of the theorem which bears his name) in southern Italy in the 6th century B.C. Their school of philosophy attempted to explain the world around them in terms of mathematical relationships. They believed that numbers were the key to the universe. The discovery of the mathematical relationships between the notes of the octave was one of their first successes, and a fruitful one, too, for it led to the theory of the music of the spheres. And whatever astronomers may now think, poets have found inspiration in it ever since. Perhaps its most familiar statement is in Lorenzo's speech to Jessica, on the lawns at Belmont in the quiet of the evening:

> Look how the floor of heaven
> Is thick inlaid with patines of bright gold;
> There's not the smallest orb which thou beholdest
> But in his motion like an angel sings,
> Still quiring to the young-eyed cherubins:
> Such harmony is in immortal souls,
> But whilst this muddy vesture of decay
> Doth grossly close it in, we cannot hear it.

MERCHANT OF VENICE, V, *1*, 58–65

Each sphere, then, revolves in a perfect circle at a constant speed, because this is the purest form of motion: there is no beginning and no end, no slowing down or speeding up. A circle is a symbol of eternity, as it later was to Henry Vaughan:

> I saw eternity the other night
> Like a great *Ring* of pure and endless light,
>   All calm as it was bright,

And round beneath it, Time in hours, days, years
　　Driven by the spheres
Like a vast shadow moved. . . . THE WORLD I–6

In fact, the whole of the heavens above the sphere of the Moon is perfect and changeless, and could be seen to be so. There are, it is true, apparent irregularities in the movements of the planets, but they can be accounted for without assuming imperfection in the heavens.

The first recorded observation which was clearly inconsistent with the theory of the perfection and immutability of the heavens was the appearance of a new star in the constellation of Cassiopeia in November 1572, which was caused by the explosion into life of what astronomers now call a *nova*. This showed that the old theory was no longer tenable. But by this time it was doomed. Copernicus, who was to be the first to use an astronomical telescope and so open the heavens to closer observations, was eight years old. And Kepler, who was to work out mathematically the laws governing the movements of the planets, was one year old at that time.

The Earth, on the other hand, was always considered to be subject to change. Common sense demanded that. One has only to look around to see change and imperfection everywhere. The weather changes hourly, while the seasons have a regular yearly cycle. Living things grow old and die; new generations are being born continually and take their place. Even inanimate objects change. A hillside may collapse in a landslide, or a river may build new land from silt it has carried downstream. However, as we shall see, the Earth is made of the four elements, earth, water, air and fire, while the heavens are made of the purer and more refined ether. Everything on Earth is subject to change and decay while all above is perfect and changeless. Hence the Earth is said to be under the Moon:

Tho gan I loke aboute and see
That ther come entryng into the halle
A ryght gret companye withalle,
And that of sondry regiouns, *various*

Of alleskynnes condiciouns   *of every state of life*
That dwelle in erthe under the mone,
Pore and ryche.

HOUSE OF FAME 1526–32

And this has rather more force than the expression 'everything under the sun', because of the connotations of imperfection and mutability. Nor are Donne's 'dull sublunary lovers' half-crazed morons.

ASTROLOGY

There is, however, a grain of comfort to be found in the mutability of this world; what comes to pass happens not at the blind dictates of pure chance. On the contrary, everything is controlled by a combination of heavenly influences, which, if one has the skill, can be calculated, just as a civil engineer can calculate the stresses in a bridge and find out whether it will be safe before it is even built. Here we leave the province of astronomy and enter upon the kindred science of astrology—for it *was* considered a science then; it had as much success in explaining people's behaviour as psychology does today. Now it survives mainly in a debased form: many popular newspapers and magazines print what they call horoscopes, which we all deny in public and read avidly in private. Here is one taken quite at random from a woman's magazine:

CAPRICORN

Friends whose interests and background differ from yours will make life much more exciting; because of them you will be launching out in new directions. All goes well on the emotional side of your life but money is a problem.

These statements are vague enough to come true in sufficient number to prove the skill of the astrologer. Medieval astrology, however, claimed to be able to give far more precise answers not only to questions of human behaviour but literally on everything under the Sun, or at least under the Moon; and because the human race is incurably curious about the future, popular belief has still not discarded the notion that the stars can affect us.

Even the Church did not condemn astrology out of hand, though she did discourage certain applications. St. Thomas Aquinas argues that the heavenly bodies are the cause of physical events in this world, and clearly says (leaving aside his proof) that 'the movements of bodies here below . . . must be referred to the movements of the heavenly bodies as to their cause' (*Summa* 1a, cxv, Art. 3). He means here physical bodies, or things, but in the next article he shows that our human bodies also must be affected by the stars. However, our bodies may be affected but our will and reason cannot be, and so even if the weak succumb to the tendencies induced by the stars, 'nothing prevents a man from resisting his passions by his free choice', and thus 'the wise man is stronger than the stars', as the astrologers themselves realize (*Summa* 1a, cxv, Art. 4). In fact, says Aquinas, astrological predictions ought to be treated like actuarial predictions today, which give a man's expectation of life but cannot tell him the day of his death. That was the Church's view, but astrology was older than the Church, and the public demanded specific predictions, which of course they got.

To discover how these predictions were made we must go back to astronomy for a while and consider the actual movements of the stars and planets, for their influence varied with their relative positions in the sky. Now this is even harder for us in the 20th century to understand than the nine crystal spheres. Let us try to see it as Chaucer would have done, forgetting all we know about our solar system of planets, including our own Earth, orbiting the Sun; let us actually use our eyes.

The first thing to grasp is that the *Stellatum* (the sphere of the fixed stars), revolves round the Earth from east to west in just under twenty-four hours—in 23 hours 56 seconds, to be exact. You can check for yourself as Chaucer could; for if he went out at exactly midnight on Monday, he would see a given constellation due south in the sky: but on Tuesday this same constellation would be a little (about one degree of radius) farther towards the west, and in a month's time the midnight sky would have drifted to the west by about thirty degrees. In a complete year, therefore, the constellation he first saw in the south at midnight would have come right round the sky (having of course been *under* the Earth at night for part of that year, and therefore invisible to him) and would be back in the same place.

Thus the background of stars is continually changing: their relative positions remain the same, but all the time some are setting in the west while others are rising in the east. But there are some heavenly bodies which do move in relation to the stars and to each other. They are the seven planets, or wanderers (for that is what the word 'planet' means). They include the Sun and Moon, but not Uranus, Neptune and Pluto which are not visible to the naked eye and so had not yet been discovered. Their spheres revolve between the *Stellatum* and the Earth at various different speeds, so that when we look out from the centre they *appear* to move against the background of the fixed stars. For six of them it is a matter of direct observation; for the most important one, the Sun, it is a little harder because its rays obscure the stars. However, since at midnight the Sun's position is diametrically opposite its position at noon, and as the stars are on the inside surface of a hollow sphere we have only to note the point of the heavens which is due north at midnight at the same height above the horizon as the Sun was at noon and find the place diametrically opposite it. It will be found that the Sun follows a circular path at an angle of twenty-three degrees to the celestial equator. In technical words, the Sun's path is called the *eccentric* and the celestial equator the *equinoctial*. It will be found, too, that the other planets, though their speeds of rotation are different, never stray more than eight degrees from the eccentric.

It is this narrow band of the heavens within which the planets move that is of the greatest interest to astrologers. It is divided into twelve equal segments, each of thirty degrees named after nearby constellations. It gets its name of *Zodiac* because several of these constellations are named after animals (Greek *zoon*= animal). The Sun takes a whole year to go round the Zodiac and come back to the sign in which it started its journey; this means that it stays in each sign for about a month at a time; and the other planets stay for a longer or shorter time depending on the speed at which they move round the Earth.

Now all this could be observed from the Earth; and as it is not unreasonable to suppose that, as the Sun could give life to the whole Earth and as the Moon could rule the tides, so the other planets could in their turn influence the lives of men and animals. Mars, for instance, could be seen to be red in colour, as blood is: it was quite logical, therefore, to associate it with war; and his influence would be increased or decreased according to what sign of the Zodiac he was occupying.

But let Chaucer explain this in his own words. He wrote a treatise on the astrolabe, an instrument for calculating the positions of the planets—we might almost call it an astronomer's slide rule. In this treatise, which is interesting not for its literary merit but for its scientific content, he tells us about the Zodiac:

> And this forseide hevenysshe zodiak is clepid the cercle of the signes, or the cercle of the bestes, for 'zodia' in langage of Grek sowneth [*means*] 'bestes' in Latyn tunge. And in the zodiak ben the 12 signes that han names of bestes, or ellis for whanne the sonne entrith into eny of tho signes he takith the propirte of suche bestes, or ellis that for the sterres that ben ther fixed ben disposid in signes of bestes or shape like bestes, or ellis whan the planetes ben under thilke signes thei causen us by her influence operaciouns and effectes like to the operaciouns of bestes.

TREATISE ON THE ASTROLABE I, 21, 50–62

Here are set down the twelve signs together with the symbols that were sometimes used to denote them. In order they are:

Aries	(Ram)	♈
Taurus	(Bull)	♉
Gemini	(Twins)	♊
Cancer	(Crab)	♋
Leo	(Lion)	♌
Virgo	(Virgin)	♍
Libra	(Scales)	♎
Scorpio	(Scorpion)	♏
Sagittarius	(Archer)	♐
Capricornus	(Goat)	♑
Aquarius	(Water Carrier)	♒
Pisces	(Fishes)	♓

Each sign has a different effect upon events on Earth. This is because they all have their own characteristics, and because various parts of the body, regions of the Earth and planets and trees are thought of as being particularly under the influence of different signs. Take Aries:

> Aries is a sign hot and dry that governeth the head of man and the face, and the regions Babylon, Persia, and Araby. And signifieth small trees. . . . They that be born under her constellation be in danger of prison or to die in prison, but if [*unless*] a good planet take regard they escape not death and prison.

This extract, slightly modernized, comes from the *Kalendar and Compost of Shepherds*, which is a late 15th-century equivalent of *Old Moore's Almanac* without the predictions but including a section on 'salutary science' which gives a course of instruction on the vices and virtues. Other authorities give different accounts of the characteristics of the signs. This is not altogether surprising, since the science of astrology had a long history, and there were as many schools of thought as there are in modern psychology. The one point they all agree on is that each sign differs in its effects on earthly affairs.

But unless the relative importance of the signs varied there would be less difference between individual people's characters, because each sign would have equal influence. Now the heavens are divided also into twelve parts, just as the Zodiac is divided into its twelve signs. Like the signs of the Zodiac there are six of the twelve divisions, or houses, under the Earth and six in the visible part above the horizon. The houses do not move, but are a fixed frame of reference against which the movements of the signs of the Zodiac and the planets can be plotted. But also each house is concerned with different aspects of the life of the person whose horoscope is being cast. The first house is the most important. It governs the general course of a person's life, or rather it is the heavenly bodies which are found in the first house at the moment of birth which control that person's destiny. The first house is the part of the sky that is just below the horizon in the east. The stars that are in it are just about to rise above the horizon.

For this reason it is known as the ascendant. Thus if somebody is said to be born under Aries, it means that he was born during the two hours each day just before Aries rises over the eastern horizon. So, because each sign is in the ascendant for only two hours at a time, it becomes important to know the exact moment of birth. Given this, it then becomes possible, with the aid of tables, like those the astrologer in the *Franklin's Tale* had, to calculate the position of all the stars and planets at the relevant moment. The horoscopes in newspapers and magazines today are useless (by medieval standards) because they cannot take into account calculations like these. Instead, they follow a rival theory that considers that the sign which the Sun occupied at the moment of birth is the one which controls that person's destiny. But as the Sun is in one sign for a month at a time, this would mean that everybody born during that month would have exactly the same characteristics—which, as Euclid said, is absurd.

INFLUENCE OF THE PLANETS

Another reason why the newspaper horoscopes are totally inadequate is that they fail to take into account the influence of the planets, which are the other main influence on men and their affairs. Like the signs of the Zodiac, each planet has its own attributes and influences. Each, too, is associated with a metal, as the Canon's Yeoman explains:

> The bodyes sevene eek, lo! hem heere anoon:
> Sol gold is, and Luna silver we threpe,   *name*
> Mars iren, Mercurie quyksilver we clepe,   *call*
> Saturnus leed, and Juppiter is tyn,
> And Venus coper, by my fader kyn!

CT: CANON'S YEOMAN'S TALE VIII, 825–9

These metals hint at the characters of the planets which are connected with them. Taking them, not in the Canon's Yeoman's order, but in order of their positions in the heavens, we come first to Saturn, the highest of the planets, and consequently the one with the widest orbit.

Saturn, like lead, is cold, dull and heavy. Because he is so far from the Sun he is a failing planet, associated with sickness and old age. He is therefore portrayed as an old man, with a crooked staff, like Old Father Time. He is a malevolent planet, and his power is increased by the size of his orbit. Because he is the most unlucky of all the planets in his influence on men, he is sometimes called *Infortuna Major*, the Greater Infortune. In history he is the cause of disastrous events, and in men of the melancholy complexion, of which more later (p. 62).

Jupiter, on the other hand, of all the planets brings the greatest luck to men. He is *Fortuna Major*, the Greater Fortune. In some accounts he is the king of all the planets. This must be a hangover from the position of Jupiter in classical mythology, where he is the ruler of all the other gods. Certainly there is a good deal of the pagan mythology left in the accounts astrologers give of the planets, for they are never entirely distinct from the old gods of the same names, and this is a case in point. (Other sources seem to give the primacy to the Sun, who is the eye and mind of the universe, who lights up all with his lifegiving beams.) Jupiter's metal is tin. Before iron became plentiful and cheap, this shining metal was greatly valued for its part in the production of bronze. If Jupiter alone had influence upon this Earth, then it would be a paradise, and men would be immortal; but as it is, other influences conspire to bring evil and decay into the world. Even so, when Jupiter is in conjunction with Saturn (that is, in the same part of the sky), and both have influence upon worldly events, he can, to some extent, mitigate Saturn's malice.

Mars, whose metal is iron, is an evil planet, second only to Saturn. He is the Lesser Infortune, *Infortuna Minor*, whose light shines red like blood, or rusty iron. He makes men iron-hard, and induces them to fight with iron weapons, for he is the planet of war. In men's affairs he causes lesser disasters than Saturn, and in men themselves he is the source of the martial temperament, as the word itself suggests.

The Sun is a lucky planet, who produces fortunate events. As might have been expected from his brightness and speed of movement across the Zodiac, he makes men fair and swift, and produces also wisdom and generosity. His metal is gold, which is really more appropriate to the chief of the planets. But as we have seen, Jupiter usually takes first place. However, as we have also seen, the Sun is called the eye and mind of the universe, which may be some consolation. Cicero called it the mind, Ovid the eye, and in this they are followed by Milton—'Thou Sun, of this great world both eye and soul' (*Paradise Lost* 5, 171).

Venus, too, is a lucky planet. She is *Fortuna Minor*, the Lesser Fortune, and is thus second only to Jupiter, though her beneficent effect is often lessened because she is frequently found in conjunction with Mars. In history she produces fortunate events, and in men beauty and amorousness. Her influence allied to that of Mars gave the Wife of Bath her character, and we will examine how this came about a little later on. Her metal is copper. This is probably another example of the close associations between the classical gods and the planets which bear their names. In Latin, copper is *cyprium*, the metal from Cyprus, which was the place where Venus rose from the waves.

Mercury is changeable. His influence is good in conjunction with good planets, and evil with evil ones. Drops of his metal, mercury, or quicksilver, move very fast and are almost impossible to pin down, which may explain his association with thieves and prison-breakers. But he is mainly associated with learning. The Wife of Bath puts it this way:

The children of Mercurie and of Venus	
Been in hir wirkyng ful contrarius;	*actions opposite*
Mercurie loveth wysdam and science,	*knowledge*
And Venus loveth ryot and dispence.	*debauchery and spending*

CT: WIFE OF BATH'S PROL. III, 697–700

And the most important encyclopedia of the Middle Ages, the *De Proprietatibus Rerum*, or 'On the Properties of Things', of Bartholomaeus Anglicus, adds that he makes men studious and lovers of sciences and all kinds of knowledge: therefore poets speak of him as the god of fair speaking and wisdom.

At the level of the Moon we come down to the great divide we mentioned earlier. The Moon looks like a great disk of silver hanging in the heavens: a metal that tarnishes as easily as silver is appropriate for the sublunary region of change and decay. She causes wandering, of wits as well as bodies. Her subjects are great

Dc

travellers, but are also prone to lunacy, that periodic madness which comes and goes with the phases of the Moon.

The influences of the planets vary according to their positions in the heavens, so that they are different from hour to hour; but they also vary in that each hour of each day of the week, and each day itself, are also under the special influence of one or other of the planets. But these hours which the planets rule are not the same as the hours by which we measure time. They are the 'hours of the planets' or 'hours inequal' as opposed to the 'hours of the clock', or 'hours equal'.

The 'hours of the clock' do not vary from one year's end to another; there are twenty-four each of sixty minutes, in each day, reckoned from midnight to midnight. But when we measure time by the 'hours of the planets', the day runs from daybreak to daybreak, and there are twelve hours of day, followed by twelve hours of night, no matter how long the daylight actually lasts. This means that the 'hours of the planets' are the same length in the daytime as they are at night only on two days in the whole year, and these are the spring and autumn equinoxes. During the rest of the year, the lengths of day and night vary continually. In December, on the shortest day, there are just under eight hours of daylight in this country. This means that from sunrise to sunset there will be twelve hours inequal, each being as short as forty minutes of an hour of the clock. Conversely, at night, the hours inequal will be twice as long—eighty minutes by the clock. On the longest day in June, when the night is little over seven hours long by the clock, the dark hours inequal will be under forty minutes long.

The planets govern each of the hours inequal in turn. The planet which has the first hour, that is, the one after daybreak, gives its name to the day, and has rather more influence during it. This is not immediately obvious to us since the Germanic gods Tiw, Woden, Thor and Freya have taken the place of their classical counterparts, Mars, Mercury, Jupiter, and Venus, in our names for the days of the week. A French or Italian reader would understand this more easily. This is how it works: given that the first hour of *Satur*day belongs to *Saturn*, then the second will belong to Jupiter (for the planets are taken in order of their positions in the heavens: see the illustration after p. 72), the third to Mars, the fourth to the Sun, the fifth to Venus, the sixth to Mercury, and the seventh to the Moon, and so on round the clock. So Saturn rules the eighth, fourteenth and twenty-second hours, and the *Sun* rules what would be the twenty-fifth hour, the first of the next day, which accordingly is *Sun*day. This calculation can be continued right through the week, a task which can be simplified by remembering that the twenty-second hour of any day must belong to the planet which gives it its name. The result will be that the first hours of the remaining days will be found to belong to the Moon, Mars, Mercury, Jupiter and Venus in turn. And this is why the days of week run Saturday, Sunday, Monday (Lundi), Tuesday (Mardi), Wednesday (Mercredi), Thursday (Jeudi) and Friday (Vendredi). The accompanying table sets out the whole week's hours inequal: it will be a great help in following the argument of the passage on the *Knight's Tale*.

	SATURDAY	SUNDAY	LUNDI MONDAY	MARDI TUESDAY	MERCREDI WEDNESDAY	JEUDI THURSDAY	VENDREDI FRIDAY
1	Saturn	Sun	Moon	Mars	Mercury	Jupiter	Venus
2	Jupiter	Venus	Saturn	Sun	Moon	Mars	Mercury
3	Mars	Mercury	Jupiter	Venus	Saturn	Sun	Moon
4	Sun	Moon	Mars	Mercury	Jupiter	Venus	Saturn
5	Venus	Saturn	Sun	Moon	Mars	Mercury	Jupiter
6	Mercury	Jupiter	Venus	Saturn	Sun	Moon	Mars
7	Moon	Mars	Mercury	Jupiter	Venus	Saturn	Sun
8	Saturn	Sun	Moon	Mars	Mercury	Jupiter	Venus
9	Jupiter	Venus	Saturn	Sun	Moon	Mars	Mercury
10	Mars	Mercury	Jupiter	Venus	Saturn	Sun	Moon
11	Sun	Moon	Mars	Mercury	Jupiter	Venus	Saturn
12	Venus	Saturn	Sun	Moon	Mars	Mercury	Jupiter
13	Mercury	Jupiter	Venus	Saturn	Sun	Moon	Mars
14	Moon	Mars	Mercury	Jupiter	Venus	Saturn	Sun
15	Saturn	Sun	Moon	Mars	Mercury	Jupiter	Venus
16	Jupiter	Venus	Saturn	Sun	Moon	Mars	Mercury
17	Mars	Mercury	Jupiter	Venus	Saturn	Sun	Moon
18	Sun	Moon	Mars	Mercury	Jupiter	Venus	Saturn
19	Venus	Saturn	Sun	Moon	Mars	Mercury	Jupiter
20	Mercury	Jupiter	Venus	Saturn	Sun	Moon	Mars
21	Moon	Mars	Mercury	Jupiter	Venus	Saturn	Sun
22	Saturn	Sun	Moon	Mars	Mercury	Jupiter	Venus
23	Jupiter	Venus	Saturn	Sun	Moon	Mars	Mercury
24	Mars	Mercury	Jupiter	Venus	Saturn	Sun	Moon

Table to show how the hours inequal are ruled by the planets throughout the week.

The signs of the Zodiac, the influences of the planets, and the hours inequal are the three most important factors to be considered when we try to discover what effect the stars have upon human destiny. Two examples from Chaucer's own works may be found interesting. The events in the *Knight's Tale* depend largely upon planetary influences and the hours inequal, while the character of the Wife of Bath was determined by the positions of the stars at her birth, that is by the signs of the Zodiac.

The whole action of the *Knight's Tale* is determined by astrological theory. This is not accidental. The first version of the story comes from the *Thebaid*, an epic poem by the Roman poet Statius; this has the classical gods, but no astrology. The second version was the *Teseide* (Story of Theseus) of Boccaccio, which also is an epic in the grandest classical style. Chaucer has taken the story from his predecessors, but in retelling it he has made it a story of the conflict of planetary influences, of Mars and Venus against Saturn, and so has provided a motivation for the actions of the characters which would have been meaningful to his audience, even if it is lost on us.

Although there is still a certain amount of classical allusion left in the story, and at times it is not clear whether, for example, in referring to Saturn the god or the planet is intended, nevertheless the main events are all governed by the planets. Arcite is the first to hint at this at the beginning of the story, when Palamon first sets eyes on Emelye and is stricken with love:

> Fortune hath yeven us this adversitee.
> Som wikke aspect or disposicioun   *malicious*
> Of Saturne, by som constellacioun,   *conjunction of stars*
> Hath yeven us this, although we hadde it sworn;
> So stood the hevene whan that we were born.
>
> CT: KNIGHT'S TALE I, 1086–90

Arcite spoke truer than he knew, for the accident which caused his death was Saturn's doing, and, as we shall see, happened in one of Saturn's hours.

There are two other places in the *Knight's Tale* where Chaucer mentions the precise time when an event took place. The first is the escape of Palamon, which comes at the beginning of the second part. It happened just after midnight on the third night of May. In the latitude of London, where the story was written (not, of course, where it is set), at the beginning of May the nights are nine hours long. So the escape takes place in the seventh hour inequal of the night and the nineteenth of the day, which started at daybreak the previous morning, and not at the previous midnight. The next day, that is May the 4th, which started at the daybreak after the escape, is a Friday. Certainly Arcite's mood suddenly changes, and Friday, Venus' day, is we are told, always very changeable:

Right as the Friday, soothly for to telle,	
Now it shyneth, now it reyneth faste,	*is sunny*
Right so kan geery Venus overcaste	*fickle*
The hertes of hir folk; right as hir day	
Is gereful, right so chaungeth she array.	*changeable*
Selde is the Friday al the wowke ylike.	*seldom week*

CT: KNIGHT'S TALE I, 1534–9

If we take it that this day is a Friday, even though Chaucer does not say so in as many words, the escape took place during Thursday night. The twenty-second hour therefore belongs to Jupiter, which day it is, the twenty-first to Saturn, the twentieth to the Moon, and the nineteenth to Mercury, as is only fitting and proper for a gaol break (see p. 49).

The second place where we are told the time of day is the Sunday before the great tournament. The participants had arrived in the morning 'aboute pryme'. (Prime was originally the hour of the first of the church's morning services, and later came to be used as the name for the period ending at 9 a.m.) Now this took place at the beginning of May in the following year, so that there would be about fifteen hours of daylight, the length of an hour inequal would be seventy-five minutes, and the fourth hour of Sunday, that of the Moon, the patron of travellers, would run from 8.15 to 9.30 a.m. Later in this day, the time of events becomes even more important, when Palamon, Emelye and Arcite go to the temples of their gods to make their prayers. Palamon goes, while it is still night, 'Although it nere nat day by houres two', to the temple of Venus. Day has not yet broken, so it is still Sunday, in fact the twenty-third hour, which must belong to Venus, as the twenty-second belongs to the Sun:

> The thridde hour inequal that Palamon
> Bigan to Venus temple for to gon,
> Up roos the sonne, and up roos Emelye,
> And to the temple of Dyane gan hye.   *began to go*

CT: KNIGHT'S TALE I, 2271–4

Diana is the goddess of the Moon, and the first hour of the day after Sunday (*i.e.* the third after the twenty-third of the previous day) must belong to the Moon. Similarly,

> The nexte houre of Mars folwynge this,
> Arcite unto the temple walked is
> Of fierse Mars, to doon his sacrifise
> With alle the rytes of his payen wyse.

CT: KNIGHT'S TALE I, 2367–70

This is not the next hour after Emelye's visit, for that is Saturn's, but the next hour which Mars presides over, which is the fourth of the day. These calculations must have been in Chaucer's mind when he wrote this passage, because in his source, Boccaccio's *Teseide*, the order in which the three make their prayers is Arcite, Palamon, and then Emelye. Here he deliberately altered the original to fit in with astrological theory.

The descriptions of the temples to which they go are all taken from those in the *Teseide* and *Thebaid*, but here, as well as by changing the order of the visits to the temples, Chaucer has done his best to show that it is not the classical gods but the planets whose influence shapes the story. The description of the temple of Mars will serve to illustrate how he does it. The first twenty lines, down to line 2017, come straight from Boccaccio and Statius. In the main, they describe paintings of death on a grand scale. Here are:

... A thousand slayn, and nat of qualm ystorve;   *hunger   starved*
The tiraunt, with the pray by force yraft;   *snatched*
The toun destroyed, ther was no thyng laft.

CT: KNIGHT'S TALE I, 2014–16

and also various criminal activities:

Ther saugh I first the derke ymaginyng
Of Felonye, and al the compassyng;   *plotting*
The crueel Ire, reed as any gleede;   *anger red live coal*
The pykepurs, and eek the pale Drede;   *pickpocket*
The smylere with the knyf under the cloke;
The shepne brennynge with the blake smoke. . . .   *stable burning*

CT: KNIGHT'S TALE, 1995–2000

and then, at line 2018, there comes a list of mere domestic misfortunes, and some very unmartial figures:

... The hunte strangled with the wilde-beres;   *boars*
The sowe freten the child right in the cradel;   *eaten*
The cook yscalded, for al his longe ladel.
Noght was foryeten by the infortune of Marte *forgotten ill-fortune*
The cartere overryden with his carte: *run over by*
Under the wheel ful lowe he lay adoun.
Ther were also, of Martes divisioun,
The barbour, and the bocher, and the smyth,   *butcher*
That forgeth sharpe swerdes on his styth.   *anvil*

CT: KNIGHT'S TALE 2018–26

These figures are often found elsewhere as examples of followers of Mars. A 17th-century astrologer gives a particularly full list:

Generals of Armies, Colonels, Captains, or any Souldiers having Command in Armies, all manner of Souldiers, Physitians, Apothecaries, Chirurgions, Alchimists, Gunners, Butchers, Marshals, Sergeants, Bailiffs, Hang-men, Theeves, Smiths, Bakers, Armourers, Watch-makers, Tailors, Cutlers of Swords and Knives, Barbers, Dyers, Cookes, Carpenters, Gamesters, Tanners, Carriers.

CHRISTIAN ASTROLOGY, William Lilly, 67

The tournament for the hand of Emelye is the heart of the story, and here the malicious influence of 'som wikke Saturn' is felt most heavily and Arcite is shown to have spoken truer than he knew. The result was decided beforehand at a quarrel in heaven

55

between Mars and Venus, for Mars has granted Arcite's prayer for victory, and Venus Palamon's for the hand of Emelye. But since it is the victor who is to take Emelye, the two prayers would appear to be mutually exclusive. So far this might have been a squabble on Mount Olympus in a classical epic, but now Jupiter and Saturn take a hand, and they are clearly intended to represent the planets, not the gods of the same names, though they continue the conversation in the Homeric way. The quarrel is ended, not by the beneficent Jupiter, the bringer of peace, as might have been expected, but, 'al be it that it is agayn his kynde' (not in accordance with his nature), by Saturn himself, the Greater Infortune, who brings disasters and pestilences in his wake. These he lists to emphasize his powers, and by doing so shows clearly that here he is not the old classical god but the planet, and that the outcome depends upon astrological influences. The list itself is too long to quote here; it may be found at lines 2453–69. If it does nothing else, it ought to arouse suspicions when Saturn settles a quarrel, for if these lines show how he normally acts, he could only settle it in a particularly nasty way.

The tournament takes place on a Tuesday, Mars' day, and, fittingly, his protégé, Arcite, wins the day. Mars has thus granted his request, and unless Saturn can do something he will take Emelye as well. Now on a Tuesday there are three hours in particular when Saturn can act. These are the sixth, which is the one ending at midday, and the first and eighth of the night. At midday, the tournament is still undecided, but 'er the sonne unto the reste wente', that is, just before sunset, Palamon is captured and defeated. Accordingly Arcite is proclaimed victor, and rides round the lists without his helmet on, to show himself. By this time the Sun must have set and Saturn's hour had come.

> Out of the ground a furie infernal sterte,
> From Pluto sent at requeste of Saturne,
> For which his hors for fere gan to turne,   *from fear shy*
> And leep aside, and foundred as he leep. . . .   *fell*
> CT: KNIGHT'S TALE I, 2684–7

Saturn, thus, caused his fall, but the injuries were not thought to be fatal, until complications set in. The blood gathered in his chest and was corrupted, and he was unable to get rid of the accumulation of poisons. Chaucer says that the 'vertu expulsif' had failed him. What he does not add, for his audience would know it already, is that opposed to the expulsive virtue is the retentive virtue, which, in good health, should balance it exactly, and which belongs to and is ruled over by Saturn. Thus it was that Saturn caused Arcite's death, and, by doing so, gave to each of the petitioners exactly what they asked for and no more.

ASTROLOGY AND THE WIFE OF BATH

The *Knight's Tale* provides several examples of planetary influences at work in day-to-day events, but for an example of how the stars shape a person's character at birth, we have to turn to someone like the Wife of Bath, who tells us that:

> For certes, I am al Venerien
> In feelynge, and myn herte is Marcien.
> Venus me yaf my lust, my likerousnesse,   *desire   lechery*
> And Mars yaf me my sturdy hardynesse;   *toughness*
> Myn ascendent was Taur, and Mars therinne.   *Taurus (the Bull)*
> Allas! allas! that evere love was synne!
> I folwed ay myn inclinacioun
> By vertu of my constellacioun. . . .   *influence*
>   CT: WIFE OF BATH'S PROL. III, 609–16

There is not enough information here to enable us to cast her horoscope properly, but from what she says it appears as if her marital career was not entirely of her own choosing. Her faults, unlike Brutus's, lay not in herself, but in her stars. She was born under Taurus, who gave her her broad face and a tendency to affairs of the heart. But in the sign of Taurus, at the moment when she was born, there were the two planets Venus and Mars. Venus takes precedence, because Taurus is one of her 'mansions'. She is therefore the ruling planet of her birth. Venus, as we saw, is a fortunate planet who produces beauty and amorousness in her subjects. And so, to elaborate a little, the Wife of Bath ought, by rights, to have had a noble disposition, and good manners.

57

Subjects of Venus are fond of music and dancing, in fact of all that is now known as 'culture'. They like fine clothes, perfumes and all kinds of bodily adornment. In one thing alone do they sometimes tend to excess, and this is in love. They usually marry more than once, but their marriages are happy ones. There may be frequent quarrels, but they are soon made up with a kiss.

Unfortunately, Venus was not the only planet in the ascendant when the Wife of Bath was born, for Mars also was in Taurus at the time. He is, as we have seen, an unfortunate planet, the Lesser Infortune. His influence has coarsened everything about her, even if he did give her her remarkable stamina, which allowed her to wear down five husbands. The *Prologue* tells us that her face is red, and what ought to have been a shapely figure is spoilt by her broad hips, which signify excessive amorousness. Her leanings towards religion have been corrupted so that she goes to church to show off her new finery, and on pilgrimage to catch new husbands. Her fondness for fine clothes has degenerated into a love of the garish and the ostentatious, such as her scarlet stockings. Mars may even have given her the gaps between her front teeth, instead of neat ones from Venus.

All in all, her behaviour may be deplorable, but it can be explained by reference to astrological theory. In the quotation from the prologue to her tale, given above, she herself attributes it to her stars, and this to the medieval mind is a satisfying explanation. We do the same sort of thing today, only we talk in terms of psychology, not astrology, and attribute delinquency to traumas which occurred in early infancy. The theories may be different, but the frame of mind which seeks for such explanations for other people's characters and excuses for our own is the same.

MEDICINE

So far we have only explored the medieval view of the heavens, and their effect upon this world. Before we move on to consider medicine, we ought first to consider the structure of the sublunary region, for theories about medicine are not unconnected with the structure of this world, the one we inhabit.

The Elements

There is an essential unity of the primary matter, which occupies all space, and from which all things are made. This primary matter takes on various forms, which can be classified by their four basic properties. These are Hot, Cold, Dry, and Moist, and are known as the four Contraries, because they are really two pairs of opposites which cannot coexist in one object; it must be either Hot or Cold: and it must be either Dry or Moist: nothing can have three or four of these properties at the same time. It follows, then, that there are four combinations of these: Hot and Dry, Hot and Moist, Cold and Dry, Cold and Moist. These four combinations characterize the four Elements. Hot and Dry make Fire; Hot and Moist make Air; Cold and Dry make Earth; Cold and Moist make Water. These four elements—Fire, Air, Earth and Water, are not to be thought of literally as being the same as what we call fire, air, earth and water, which are no more than imperfect copies of them. The flames which we see every day are fire in an impure state: it is their impurity that makes them visible; the smoke is due to an admixture of earth. This is the generally accepted theory of the elements. Chaucer, however, in one passage implies that there are six Contraries:

> Nature, the vicaire of the almyghty Lord,   *deputy*
> That hot, cold, hevy, lyght, moyst, and dreye
> Hath knyt by evene noumbres of acord. . . .

PARLEMENT OF FOULES 379–81

This can be no more than an embellishment on Chaucer's part, for all authorities, right from the Greek philosophers of the 5th century B.C., who first propounded the theory, are agreed that there are only four elements, and Chaucer well knew this. Take the Doctor in the *Prologue* to the *Canterbury Tales*:

> He knew the cause of everich maladye,
> Were it of hoot, or coold, or moyste, or drye. . . .

CT: GEN. PROL. I, 419–20

The difference between the two passages is that, in the *Prologue*, Chaucer is showing how learned the Doctor is, and so must give the correct version of the doctrine, while in the *Parlement*, the passage quoted is not part of the argument. It is a piece of poetic decoration, which tells us something about Nature: but, all the same, in this context, the number of elements is irrelevant. Here is a warning to us perhaps against building a theory on a small piece of evidence, without first considering its context.

The Humours

In some ways, the human body is a replica in miniature of the universe. It is the microcosm, while the universe is the macrocosm, and there are many parallels between the two. So it is with the elements, for in the body the same combinations of the Contraries form the basic elements from which our bodies are made. The difference is one of name; these combinations are properly called Humours, or liquids (Latin—*humor*), not Elements. Hot and Dry make Choler; Hot and Moist, Blood; Cold and Dry, Phlegm; Cold and Moist, Melancholy. We all are made of varying combinations of these Humours, but the proportion in which they are combined is different in each individual. In any combination one Humour will predominate, and become the chief physical factor in determining that person's character. But although no two people will have exactly the same combination of Humours, the combinations will fall into one of four types, depending upon which Humour predominates.

The Complexions

The technical name for these combinations of Humours is 'Complexions'. This word did not get its modern meaning of 'facial colouring' until almost Shakespeare's time (indeed Shakespeare uses the word in both senses) so that when Chaucer says of the Franklin, 'Of his complexioun he was sangwyn', he means a good deal more than 'He had a ruddy face'. The colour of his face was only a *symptom* of his Complexion. If he had wanted to say what we understand by 'complexion', he would probably have used *rode*, as he did in the *Miller's Tale* (3317): 'His rode was reed, his eyen greye as goos'. The *Kalendar and Compost of Shepherds* describes the four Complexions; it is interesting to read this popular exposition of medical science in the Middle Ages.

The Sanguine Complexion

The sanguine hath nature of air, hot and moist. He is large, plenteous attempered, amiable, abundant in nature, merry, singing, laughing, liking, ruddy and gracious. He hath his wine of the ape, more he drinketh the merrier he is, and draweth to women and naturally loveth high coloured cloth.   KALENDAR Ch. 29

One thing is missing from this list: the Sanguine man is also rather short-tempered, even though his anger does not last long.

The Choleric Complexion

The choleric hath nature of fire, hot and dry, naturally is lean and slender, covetous, ireful, hasty, brainless, foolish, malicious, deceitful, and subtle where he applieth his wit. He hath wine of the lion, that is to say, when he is drunken he chideth, fighteth, and commonly he loveth to be clad in black, as russet and grey.

KALENDAR Ch. 29

Bartholomaeus Anglicus, here in a 14th-century translation, agrees, and also shows where the anger comes from.

Colerik men been generally wrathful, in ye body longe and sklendre and lene. . . . Mars hath maystery over colera, fyre and coleryk complexion; he disposeth the soule . . . to wrathe . . . and to other coleryke passions.

The description of the Reeve in the *Prologue* bears all this out, both in appearance:

The Reeve was a sclendre colerik man . . . .
Ful longe were his legges and ful lene,
Ylyk a staf, ther was no calf ysene.

CT: GEN. PROL. I 587–92

and in behaviour, as the quotation on page 20 shows.

The Phlegmatic Complexion

The phlegmatic hath nature of water, cold and moist. He is heavy, slow, sleepy, ingenious, commonly he spitteth when he is moved, and hath his wine of the sheep, for when he is drunken he accounteth himself wisest, and he loveth most green colour.

KALENDAR Ch. 29

Phlegm causes constitutional indolence and apathy, or as Bartholomaeus puts it:

A very flewmatike man is in the body lustles, heuy and slow.

Such men are nature's dullards, in fact, exactly what we colloquially mean by 'thick', for their bodies are as fat as their wits are slow. It appears that Milton found himself married to such a woman, for almost as soon as he had married Mary, his first wife, after a whirlwind courtship, he published a pamphlet advocating divorce in which he expresses his sympathy for the man who 'shall find himself bound fast to an image of earth and phlegm'.

The Melancholy Complexion

The melancholic hath nature of earth, cold and dry. He is heavy, covetous, backbiter, malicious, and slow. His wine is of the hog, for when he is drunken he desireth sleep, and to lie down. And he loveth of black colour.   KALENDAR Ch. 29

A melancholy man suffers from rather more than an occasional fit of sadness or depression. 'Melancholy' did not begin to mean 'sad' or 'introverted, thoughtful' until the 16th century. Rather the melancholy man is what we would now call a neurotic. Hamlet, for example, is liable to sudden outbursts of involuntary and ungovernable rage or excitement. He has half a dozen of these, and they alternate with periods of extreme tenderness. He is clearly an unstable character. Claudius puts it down to 'turbulent lunacy', but Hamlet himself, at the end of Act II, Scene 2, diagnoses himself as melancholy.

Health and the Humours

So far we have only been considering the way in which a person's character depends on the Humours, but this is not the only item which they determine, for good health depends upon the proper proportion between the Humours being maintained. Once there is too much of any of the Humours, ill health is the result. In the *Nun's Priest's Tale*, Chauntecleer is lucky only to get nightmares from his superfluity of choler and melancholy. The Summoner and the Cook both came off worse; although Chaucer does not say so, the Summoner's skin disease was probably due to a corruption of blood, and the Cook's mormal, or ulcer, to a corruption of melancholy.

But the Humours also vary according to the time of day, of month, and of year, without causing disease. These fluctuations must be taken into account in any treatment. In every day each Humour is dominant for six hours at a time: blood from midnight to 6 a.m.; choler, from 6 a.m. to noon; melancholy, from noon to 6 p.m.; finally phlegm, from then up to midnight. In each month the strength of all the Humours varies with the phases of the Moon, being greatest when the Moon is fullest. Thirdly, each season of the year has affinities with one of the Humours;

> Prime (Spring) time is hot and moist, nature of air, and complexion of the sanguine. Summer is hot and dry, nature of fire, and complexion of choleric. Harvest (Autumn) is cold and dry, nature of earth, and complexion of melancholy. Winter is cold and moist, nature of water, complexion of the phlegmatic. KALENDAR Ch. 17

Health and the Heavens

Besides the hourly variations in the Humours, a doctor would take careful note of the position of the heavens, because the signs of the Zodiac and the planets have influence over the way our bodies work as well as over our characters and actions. Each sign and planet has the nature of one of the four elements, so that, for instance, Aries, Leo, Sagittarius, and Mars are hot and dry like Fire, while Taurus, Virgo, Capricorn and Saturn are cold and dry like Earth. Furthermore, each of these zodiacal signs rules a part of the human body:

> The first, that is Aries, governeth the head and face of man; Taurus, the neck and the throatball; Gemini, the shoulders, the arms, and the hands; Cancer, the breast, sides, milt, and lights; Leo, the stomach, the heart, and back; Virgo, the belly and the entrails: Libra, the navel, the groins, the parts under the branches; Scorpio, the privy parts, the genitals, the bladder, and the fundaments; Sagittarius, the thighs only; Capricorn, the knees only, also; Aquarius, the legs and from the knees to the heels and ankles; and Pisces hath the feet in his dominion. KALENDAR Ch. 13

That is just a straightforward list. We can see the theory being applied, albeit inaccurately, by Sir Andrew Aguecheek and Sir Toby Belch in *Twelfth Night*:

SIR ANDREW: Shall we set about some revels?
SIR TOBY: What shall we do else? Were we not born under Taurus?
SIR ANDREW: Taurus? That's sides and heart.
SIR TOBY: No, sir; it is legs and thighs. Let me see thee caper.

TWELFTH NIGHT I, 3, 127–31

Likewise the planets also rule parts of the body: Saturn, the spleen; Jupiter, the liver; Mars, the gall bladder; the Sun, the heart; Venus, the kidneys; Mercury, the lungs; the Moon, the head. Four of the planets govern the Humours, and one of these, the Moon, has influence over all four together. Blood belongs to the Sun; choler to Mars; melancholy to Saturn; phlegm to the Moon.

Treatments

With all this to consider, it is no wonder that Chaucer mentions the Doctor's skill in astronomy:

With us ther was a Doctour of Phisik;	
In al this world ne was ther noon hym lik,	
To speke of phisik and of surgerye,	
For he was grounded in astronomye.	
He kept his pacient a ful greet deel	*did things at the right time*
In houres by his magyk natureel.	*[of the planets*
Wel koude he fortunen the ascendent	*find the favourable positions*
Of his ymages for his pacient.	
He knew the cause of everich maladye,	
Were it of hoot, or coold, or moyste, or drye,	
And where they engendred, and of what humour.	*arose*
He was a verray, parfit praktisour:	*true practitioner*
The cause yknowe, and of his harm the roote,	*when he knew*
Anon he yaf the sike man his boote.	*remedies*

CT: GEN. PROL. I, 411–24

For only when the stars were in the right places would his remedies have any effect. His aim would be to get rid of the excess of the Humours which were causing the disease. He had two methods at hand. The first of these was by letting blood; the amount taken and the place from which it comes determine the effect. For instance, according to the *Kalendar*:

> The vein in the middle of the forehead would be let blood for the ache and pain of the head, and for fevers, lethargy, and for the megrim.

This seems reasonable; but some of the other places specified are rather less expected:

> In each hand be three veins wherof that above the thumb ought to be bled to take away the great heat of the visage, and for much thick blood and humours that be in the head; this vein evacueth more than that of the arm.   KALENDAR Ch. 15

Blood-letting was particularly important to clear the bad Humours which had accumulated during the winter, but it had its limitations. Because the Moon had such an effect on the Humours (which is shown by the way they vary with its phases), it was very dangerous to bleed the part of the body which was ruled by the sign of the Zodiac that the Moon happened to be in at that time, for fear that the Moon would draw the Humours to that part and cause a serious infection. Secondly, in the second and fourth quarters of the Moon the Humours are withdrawn towards the interior of the body, and so prevent letting.

The second method of treatment was by administering drugs to purge the unwanted Humours. This is the method employed by Dame Pertelote, when, in the *Nun's Priest's Tale*, Chauntecleer is troubled by a dream, which she attributes, as with all dreams, to excess of some Humour:

> Certes this dreem, which ye han met to-nyght,   *dreamed*
> Cometh of the greete superfluytee
> Of youre rede colera. . . .   *red choler*
>   CT: NUN'S PRIEST'S TALE VII 2926-8 (B4116-18)

He must prepare the way for purgatives by taking a digestive for a day or so, or else he will run the risk of a tertian fever if he goes out in the sun with all his hot choler. This is all standard medical practice, except that Pertelote does not mention the need to take these medicines at the favourable hour. The purgatives, too, though apparently all growing close at hand, are standard medicines of the time. At first glance, Chaucer seems to have inserted one item particularly appropriate to the fowls who are the subject of this tale:

> A day or two ye shul have digestyves
> Of wormes, er ye take youre laxatyves. . . .
> CT: NUN'S PRIEST'S TALE VII, 2961-2 (B4151-2)

But even worms are a standard medical remedy for men and women! Dioscorides, in his standard work, *De Materia Medica*, prescribes them for tertian fevers. Chauntecleer was perhaps lucky that as a fowl he could take them straight; for human consumption they should be boiled with goose-grease, or prepared as a decoction in oil, or ground up and taken with food.

Once the doctor had given the appropriate treatment at the hour at which it would do most good, he could go one step farther and make the favourable astrological influences permanent by embodying them in a seal or medal to be carried on the person; for inanimate objects, as well as men, are permanently influenced by the stars at the moment of their creation. It would take a long time to produce one to fit a special situation, because each stage has to be carried out when the heavens are in the right position, so some authorities describe how to make twelve stock medals, one for each sign of the Zodiac. This is how to make one valid in Aries, according to Arnaldus de Villanova, who lived a century before Chaucer:

> Take purest gold, and let it be melted as the sun is entering the Ram. Then let there be modelled of it a round seal, and while it is being moulded into a round you shall say: Rise, light of the world, Jesu true lamb who bearest the sins of the world, and lighten our darkness. . . . And when it is made, then let it be laid away. And

after the Moon enters Cancer or Leo, let there be graven on one side the figures of a ram, while the sun is in the Ram, and about the circumference Arahel tribus Juda, quinque et septem. And on the other side, about the circumference, let these most sacred words be graven: The word was made flesh and dwelt amongst us. And in the middle, Alpha and Omega and Sanctus Petrus.

The Bedside Manner

In the *Prologue*, Chaucer tells us of the Doctor's learning, and I have tried to explain what it entailed in the last few pages. He also tells us of his good clothes and his fondness for money:

In sangwyn and in pers he clad was al,	*red blue-grey*
Lyned with taffata and with sendal;	*thin silk*
And yet he was but esy of dispence;	*slow to spend*
He kepte that he wan in pestilence.	*took in times of plague*
For gold in phisik is a cordial	
Therefore he lovede gold in special.	

CT: GEN. PROL. I, 439–44

Now some scholars, in their search for a model for Chaucer's portrait of the Doctor, have come across, amongst others, a certain John of Arderne, who is remembered for his treatise *De Fistula in Ano*, which he wrote in 1376. He may well have known Chaucer, for he was surgeon to John of Gaunt, Chaucer's patron. But whether he did or not, and whether or not he was the model for the Doctor, are really immaterial; the interest from our point of view comes from his treatise, which he intersperses with advice on professional conduct. A doctor should be studious:

And be he euermore occupied in thingis that beholdith to his crafte; outhir rede he or studie he, or write or pray he; for the excercyse of bokes worshippeth [*brings honour to*] a leche.

DE FISTULA, John of Arderne,* 4, 21

and soberly dressed:

Also dispose a leche hym that in clothes and in othir apparalyngis be he honeste, noght likkenyng hymself in apparalyng or berying to mynistralles, but in clothing and beryng shew he the manner

---

* E.E.T.S. OS.139.

of clerkes. ffor why; it semeth any discrete man y-cladde with clerkis clothing for to occupie gentil mennes bordes [*tables*].

6, 26

He should come to an agreement about his fee, which should not be too small, before he operates:

> And yif he se the pacient persewe bisily the cure, than after that the state of the pacient asketh aske he boldly more or lesse; but euer be he warre of scarse askyngis, ffor ouer scarse askyngis setteth at not both the markette and the thing.

5, 37

The fee he actually suggests is forty pounds, a robe and a yearly annuity of five pounds, from a well-to-do patient. For those who are less well off he will forgo the annuity, but in no case is he prepared to operate for less than five pounds. It is difficult to translate these figures into present-day values, but they are clearly very high. Chaucer's own annuity from Richard II was twenty pounds. It is not surprising that John of Arderne recommends the surgeon to ask for half in advance:

> And than acord thay of couenant, of whiche couenant—all excusacione y-put abak—take he half byfore handes.

15, 29

Still working on the same principles as determined the size of the fee, he advises against giving the rich cheap medicines. Maybe those who suggest that Chaucer's Doctor used *aurum potabile* (gold in cordial, drinkable gold) to put the price of his medicines up were not so far wrong:

> But witte thou that to worthi men and to noble it semeth [*is fitting*] to putte to more noble medicines and more dere.

25, 16

ALCHEMY

Astrology and Medicine are the two most important of the medieval sciences, and we have dealt with them at some length because they affected everyone. Astrology was ingrained in popular belief and was thus part of the climate of opinion; while Medicine is obviously of general concern.

The third science we must consider is Alchemy. It differs from the others in that it was a mystery, a secret into which one had to be initiated. It took its origins in Egypt from the trade practices of craftsmen. That is, it started as chemical technology, rather than as chemistry, as is generally supposed. These Egyptian craftsmen were able to produce imitations of precious metals and stones, and substitutes for expensive dyes like the purple produced by *murex*, a shellfish that was expensive to gather and transport. The craftsmen had no intention to deceive by proclaiming that they were producing the real thing; like chainstore jewellery today, their wares were cheaper and did not wear as well as the real thing, but they were not unlike it. They either produced cheap alloys or coloured base metals with pigments, such as the famous *orpiment* (arsenic trisulphide). Similarly, they made jewels from coloured glass or added coloured coatings: a topaz covered with verdigris looked like an emerald—for a short time. In the production of their imitations they made great use of the processes of distillation.

Just as the practice started in Egypt, so did the theory and, in Egypt, Greek learning and Egyptian know-how came together. This is where the mysticism crept in. The classical Greek school of philosophers and their followers were unique until modern times in that their learning had no link with religion. Aristotle provided one of the fundamental tenets: that all things are in a process of change and development. We can see this particularly clearly in living things. But minerals too are changing, and it is only the slowness at which they develop that prevents us from watching them growing in the womb of the earth. Alchemists attempted to imitate and accelerate these natural processes of growth and change in the laboratory, especially with the aid of a catalyst—the Philosopher's Stone, that mythical element which was the object of their profoundest search. Their other line of attack was to seed the mixture of baser metals with a small piece of the substance—say, gold—which they wished to produce in large quantities, and thus encourage it to grow, like yeast, or a cultured pearl.

The second fundamental tenet or premise was that matter was

inhabited by spirit which controlled its form and body, its bulk and outward expression. When a log burns, for instance, the spirit passes from it with the smoke and flames, and the amorphous body, losing its shape with the departure of the spirit, falls to ashes. There were four spirits, made up of the four elements and the four qualities, thus tying alchemy into the structure of the universe. The alchemists' hope was that if only it were possible to synthesize by distillation the spirit—or essence—that makes gold gold, it would be possible to produce gold at will.

When these ancient theories of matter came into contact with the Christian belief in redemption by regeneration, the way was open to the development of alchemy into an occult mystery, and the consequent camouflage of all discussion of it under a cloud of jargon (Ben Jonson's play *The Alchemist* contains the best known examples of this secret 'scientific' language in our literature). But as far as we can tell, the actual practice was rather like this: since there are six metals, all of which contain varying quantities of the two spirits, mercury and sulphur, any base metal can be transmuted into a higher one by altering proportions of the spirit with the Philosopher's Stone as a catalyst. This process must take place in two parts: firstly to remove the impurities, and secondly to make up what has been lost, to raise the purified metal to a higher state, by 'projecting' the Stone on to it.

The main reference to alchemy in Chaucer comes in the *Canon's Yeoman's Tale*, which is a cautionary tale directed against those who dupe themselves and those who try to dupe others. For the practice of alchemy was a chancy business with plenty of scope for trickery. At the end, however, Chaucer seems to recommend the true alchemy for its spiritual value once the charlatans are dismissed.

One small point here is that the *Canon's Yeoman's Tale*, in opposition to what is said above, classes mercury as a metal, not a spirit. This serves to emphasize the difficulty of explaining the beliefs and practices of such a remote and strange mode of thought, in a clear and incontrovertible manner; but we must also remember that even modern scientific theories can be mutually contradictory.

4

Books and Learning

In Chapter 1 we looked at the social background of Chaucer's works; but one major facet of this we did not explore: the position of the writer, the conditions of book production and the likely readership he was catering for and could hope for. Today, a successful author is well rewarded by society: Ian Fleming, creator of James Bond and possibly the most successful writer of recent years, sold a proportion of the rights of his books for £1½ millions—so lavishly do we pay for our entertainment these days when film and television rights bring an author's creations to a world-wide audience.

But few writers could support themselves by writing in the 14th century. As his life shows, Chaucer was not a professional writer, making his living by his pen. He was a full-time civil servant for most of his life who had to fit his writing into what time was left when his duties were done. He is not the only civil servant in English Literature: nearer our own time Matthew Arnold was one of Her Majesty's Inspectors of Schools, and Anthony Trollope held a similar position in the Post Office.

Chaucer, however, did not have the choice of making his living by his pen. It was not until considerably later that a writer's work was thought to be his exclusive property which could be bought and sold. Furthermore, until the invention of printing it was physically impossible to produce a large number of identical copies of a book for sale reasonably cheaply. Until the end of the 15th century, each copy of a book had had to be laboriously written out by hand. In 1475, less than a hundred years after Chaucer began the *Canterbury Tales*, the first book in the English language left the printing press. The printer was

Caxton and the place was Bruges. He seems to have taken printing up as a sideline, for the first part of his life was spent as a merchant in Bruges, not without considerable success. However, when he was not far short of fifty years old, with the encouragement of Margaret, the sister of Edward IV, he turned to translating a French account of the *History of Troy*. The translation became so popular in his circle that he tired of copying it out for his friends. But he fortunately had taken advantage of a stay in Cologne to learn printing, and in 1475, a couple of years after his return to Bruges, with the assistance of Colard Mansion, he produced the *Recuyell of the Histories of Troy*: his epilogue to the 3rd Book says:

> Therfore I haue practysed and lerned at my charge and dispense to ordeyne this said book in prynte after the maner and forme as ye may here see, and is not wreton with penne and ynke as other bokes ben, to thende that euery man may have them attones, for all the bookes of this storye named the recule of the historyes of troyes thus empryntid as ye here see were begonne in oon day, and also fynyshid in oon day.
>
> PROLOGUES AND EPILOGUES, Caxton*

This is exaggeration: he could not possibly have printed the *Recuyell* in a single day. However, he was now able to produce multiple copies of his works much more easily than by writing them out by hand. And what is more, there must have been a market ready for them, as he went on to publish some ninety books, mostly in English, including the *Canterbury Tales*. His successor, Wynkyn de Worde, was even more prolific; he published over 800 works before 1535.

Although Caxton broke new ground by printing his books, in other ways he was no different from other authors of the time, and even though he did use print, the finished product looks very much like a handwritten book. Firstly, he was not a professional. He was a successful business man, just as Chaucer was a civil servant, and as was Hoccleve a little later, who spent his life as a clerk in the Office of the Privy Seal. John Gower, Chaucer's

* E.E.T.S. OS.176.

Es nouuelles Albion
Sil vous en plaist escouter
Mon frere e mon compaignio
Sachiez qua mon retonier
Ly este sera sa mer
E ceu a joyeuse cheire

Charles d'Orleans shown in three places in the Tower of London. Notice London Bridge in the background

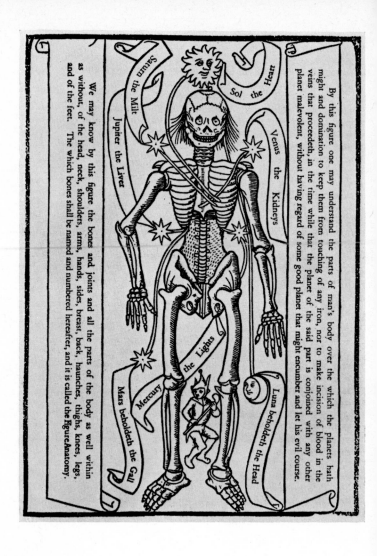

By this figure one may understand the parts of man's body over the which the planets hath might and domination to keep them from touching of any iron, nor to make incision of blood in the veins that proceedeth, in the time while that the planet of the said part is conjoined with any other planet malevolent, without having regard of some good planet that might encumber and let his evil course.

Sol the Heart

Saturn the Milt

Jupiter the Liver

Venus the Kidneys

Mars beholdeth the Gall

Mercury the Lights

Luna beholdeth the Head

We may know by this figure the bones and joints and all the parts of the body as well within as without, of the head, neck, shoulders, arms, hands, sides, back, haunches, thighs, knees, legs, and of the feet. The which bones shall be named and numbered hereafter, and it is called the Figure Anatomy.

A 15th-century diagram showing the relationship between the planets and parts of the body

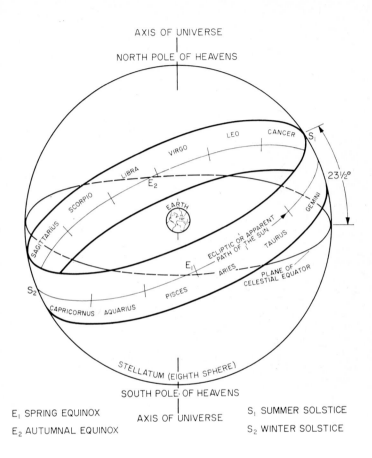

A plan showing the position of the heavenly bodies. Imagine seven spheres, one for each planet, between the Earth and the Stellatum, each with the Earth at its centre

A good example of Gothic art is this altarpiece by a 13th-century Aachen master, showing the story of the Crucifixion

contemporary and friend, had independent means; other authors were in Holy Orders. Froissart, the chronicler, was not the only man to be given a church living to allow him to get on with his literary work.

Then, secondly, Caxton wrote because he had the encouragement and support of a patron, in his case the King's sister. Gower, too, received the royal command from Richard II, who met him on the Thames and, inviting him into the royal barge:

> He hath this charge upon me leid,
> And bad me doo my besynesse
> That to his hihe worthinesse
> Som newe thing I scholde boke,
> That he himself it mihte loke
> After the forme of my writynge.
> And thus upon his comandynge
> Myn herte is wel the more glad
> To write so as he me bad.

CONFESSIO AMANTIS Prol. 48–56

Not all authors had such august patronage. For one thing, most had only a local reputation. Before printing made possible the nation-wide distribution of books, and improved communications made newspapers possible, the only way an author became known was by word of mouth, and by the circulation of handwritten copies of his works. Hence it is not uncommon to find several versions of a theme or translations of a story in different parts of the country. For each area the local version was the one that mattered: the others would be unknown, or even if known, probably less intelligible because of difference of dialect.

Before printing, the way books were produced was something like this: the original stimulus often came from a prospective patron. We have seen how Gower received a royal command and Caxton encouragement when his enthusiasm flagged. Chaucer had close connections with John of Gaunt: but showed them only in his early *Book of the Duchess*. And other lesser households up and down the country must have held squires whose skill at entertaining the company (see p. 13) was little less than Chaucer's, though their names are lost. One of the reasons for

Chaucer's fame must be the distinction of the circle in which he found himself: how many other 'mute inglorious Miltons' were never heard of outside their circle we shall never know.

When the author's manuscript was complete, a professional scrivener produced a presentation copy for the patron. Afterwards, people who wanted a copy for themselves would have to copy it out or employ a professional to do it for them, and the final result was quite often a book containing a hotch-potch of items related only in that they had caught the fancy of the owner. A modern book is issued in batches, all copies in the batch being identical, and revision is only possible by issuing a new edition: but a medieval author could be working on his original manuscript for years, polishing and altering it as he went along, so that a copy made from it one year might not be the same as one made the following year. The passage by Gower (quoted on p. 73) is an example of this. It appears in the first version of the *Confessio* produced about 1390; by 1393 he had fallen out with the King, so this passage no longer appears: and this is why it is not to be found in the modern translation in the Penguin Classics series. Alternatively, there is always the possibility of scribal error; professional scriveners, more concerned for the look of the page than for the sense, could be more guilty of alteration than an amateur copying a work out for his own use. Chaucer is no stranger to this, as a short poem called *Chaucer's wordes unto Adam his owne Scriveyn* shows:

Adam scriveyn, if ever it thee bifalle
Boece or Troylus for to wryten newe,   [*scab*
Under thy long lokkes thou most have the scalle, *may you have the*
But after my makyng thou wryte more trewe;   *unless*
So ofte a-daye I mot thy werk renewe,
It to correcte and eek to rubbe and scrape;
And al is thorugh thy negligence and rape.   *haste*

Until the advent of printing it was practically impossible to buy a book off the shelf. The only places where this could be done were the universities and London; by the end of the 14th century there was one stationer in business, called John Shirley, who has left his name on several surviving manuscripts which must have been part of his stock. From stanzas such as this which are found in a number of his manuscripts, it seems that his business was in part a lending library:

> Yee that desyre in herte and have plesaunce
> Olde stories in bokis for to rede
> Gode matteres putt hem in remembraunce
> And of the other take ye more hede
> Whanne yee this boke have ouer-redde and seyne
> To John Shirley restore yee hit ageyne.

His books were compilations strung together with a commentary, which was often the only reason for assigning certain works to their authors. One, now in the British Museum (MSS. Add. 16165), contains Chaucer's translation of Boethius, *Master of Game* by the second Duke of York, Lydgate's *Complaint of the Black Knight*, the *Regula sacerdotalis*, Chaucer's *Anelida*, Lydgate's *St. Anne* and *Departing of Chaucer*, the Earl of Warwick's poem to Lady Despenser, and a number of shorter poems.

EDUCATION

Such collections as this show that there was a market for books. Shirley died in 1456; less than a century later, in 1533, Sir Thomas More estimated that well over half the population were literate. This is probably an exaggeration and had certainly not been true in Chaucer's time, a century and a half before; but even then literacy must have been on the increase, as schools and colleges such as Winchester and New College were being founded up and down the country. And it would be wrong to equate literacy with the number of *English* texts that survive, for up to the 14th century literacy meant as often as not the ability to read *French*, the language of culture.

Education was originally provided to keep the services of the Church going by producing educated men and boys to take part in them. The original elementary school was the song school where the pupils were:

... Children an heep, ycomen of Cristen blood,   *crowd born*
That lerned in that scole yeer by yere   *place*
Swich manere doctrine as men used there,   *such sort of learning*
This is to seyn, to syngen and to rede,
As smale children doon in hire childhede.

CT: PRIORESS'S TALE VII, 497–501 (B1687–91)

Schools like these were attached to a cathedral or major parish church, just as choir schools are today, where the boys sing in the choir and are at the same time prepared for the public schools. The pupils in the song school, too, took part in the services, which were of course in Latin: and it must be admitted that they did so more by parrot learning than with understanding. The passage quoted above from the *Prioress's Tale* goes on to describe the fate of one of the pupils, 'a litel clergeon seven year of age', who was at a reading school attached to a song school. He heard the choir boys singing the *Alma Redemptoris Mater* and learnt it by heart, but failed to get a full explanation of it from one of them because:

I kan namoore expounde in this mateere;
I lerne song, I kan but small grammeere.   *only know*

CT: PRIORESS'S TALE VII, 535–6 (B1725–6)

What they did learn was mainly devotional; the Our Father, Hail Mary, I Confess, the Creed, Ten Commandments, the Seven Deadly Sins and a few prayers and psalms.

Grammar was taught in the secondary or grammar schools. Although these became more and more to be used as feeders to the universities as they expanded in the 13th and 14th centuries, they still remained under the control of the Church. In London there were three attached to the great parish churches of St. Martin-le-Grand, St. Mary-le-Bow, and St. Paul's Cathedral, where the schoolmaster in the middle of the century was William Ravenstone, who left his library of eighty-four books bound in forty-three volumes to the school in 1358. This was an outstanding collection for those days, when each had been written out by hand; and the twenty which Chaucer's Clerk of Oxenford possessed was a quite remarkable number. Chaucer probably attended one of the three schools, maybe even St. Paul's, with its fine library. Certainly Chaucer shows himself well read in the classics, and here, close at hand, was a fine collection.

THE SEVEN LIBERAL ARTS

To talk of grammar schools makes them sound modern but, although many, including St. Paul's, have survived from the 14th century, it would be wrong to think that the curriculum was similar to that of their modern successors. Grammar was one of the Seven Liberal Arts (called *liberal* from the Latin *liber=* free). From Plato onwards they were considered fit subjects for *freemen* to study as opposed to the Practical and Mechanical Arts which were only fit for slaves. These were the technologies which keep society running and which even now are less highly esteemed in most university circles. The Seven Liberal Arts were Grammar, Rhetoric, Dialectic (logic), Arithmetic, Geometry, Astronomy and Music. They served as an introduction to Theology, which was the Queen of the Sciences, towards which all others were directed. There developed a division of labour between the grammar schools and the universities in the teaching of the arts; the first three, the *Trivium*, were taught in the schools, and the other four, the *Quadrivium*, in the universities. Of these, Grammar was by far the most important. We get a false impression from the modern meaning of the word, which now is used in a far more restricted sense than it was originally. For the word *grammar* is etymologically equivalent to the word *literature*: the first coming from the Greek word for *letter* and the second from its Latin equivalent. From classical times until the end of the Middle Ages, Grammar included the methodical study of all aspects of literature, and this involved not only what we now call Grammar, that is the study of the rules of a language, but also dealt with style and composition, and then with literary history and criticism, and sufficient study of background material to explain the allusions. In short, Grammar provided all that was necessary for the interpretation of a text, that is, a Latin text, for Latin was the universal language of learning.

The most usual grammar book for a beginner was that written

by Donatus. His *Ars Minor* deals with the parts of speech in question and answer form:

Q. How many parts of speech are there?
A. Eight.
Q. Which are they?
A. Noun, pronoun, verb, adverb, participle, conjunction, preposition and interjection.

It then examines these eight in detail, still by means of question and answer, this being the easiest way of learning a complicated subject by heart. For treatises like this were learnt by heart—they had to be because books were scarce as long as they were written by hand. Even so, this method of teaching by dialogue lasted for many centuries, as is proved by the phenomenal success of the 16th-century scholar Cordery's *Colloquies*, which ran through many editions in the course of its hundred years of life. The shortage of books affected university teaching, so that many teachers dictated the set text to their students.

The schoolboys had also to be able to translate these grammar books, originally into French, but in Chaucer's lifetime English became the language of instruction, as John of Trevisa tells us in a paragraph he added to his translation of the *Polychronicon* of Ranulf Higden, a universal history covering from the Creation to 1327:

> For Johan Cornwal, a mayster of gramere, changede the lore in gramer-scole, and construccion of Freynsch into Englysch; and Richard Pencrych lurnede that manere techyng of hym, and other men of Pencrych; so that now, the yer of oure Lord a thousand thre hondred foure score and fyve, of the secunde kyng Richard after the conquest nyne, in al the gramer-scoles of Engelond childern leveth Frensch and construeth and lurneth an Englysch, and habbeth therby avauntage in on syde and desavauntage yn another; here avauntage ys that a lurneth here gramer yn lasse tyme than childern wer y-woned to do; disavauntage ys that now childern of gramer-scole conneth no more Frensch than can here lift heele, and that ys harm for ham, and a scholle passe the se and travayle in strange londes, and in meny caas also.

HANDBOOK OF MIDDLE ENGLISH, Mossé, 287

The *Ars Minor* of Donatus covers only a small part of the whole subject. Another branch of Grammar that is particularly important to a poet codifies the actual form and shape of written texts and thus provides a blueprint for an author to enable him to put together his works in the most telling way. Thus it overlaps the ground covered by Rhetoric, for after dealing with the forms of words, grammar books like Donatus' *Ars Grammatica*, which follows his *Ars Minor*, go on to deal with their use, and to classify and explain the tricks of the trade which give style to an expression. These are of two kinds, figures of language and figures of thought.

> There are figures both of language and thought; that, is, figures of words and of meanings. Figures of thought belong to rhetoric; to grammar figures of language. Although there are many, of all these perhaps 17 are necessary, and their names are as follows . . .
> ARS GRAMMATICA, Donatus, III, 5

The list is omitted because the words mean nothing today. Only one of them may still be found quoted in school textbooks; this is *zeugma* (a yoking together) memorable mainly for the example often given: 'She departed in a flood of tears and a sedan chair'. One which Donatus does not list he actually uses in the passage quoted; this is *chiasmus* (a crossing over) in which two halves of a sentence are mirror images of each other: 'Figures of thought belong to rhetoric; to grammar figures of language'.

RHETORIC

Rhetoric had its origins in the courthouses of antiquity; it taught the litigants how to present their cases to the best advantage. When, under the later Roman Empire, the freedom of the courts was a thing of the past, the concern of Rhetoric was transferred to literary composition in general, and came, in the end, to be no more than another word for the study of poetry. However, even before then, the manuals set out to teach a writer how to tell his story as effectively as he could. They concentrated on technique rather than on emotional content: their aim was to produce a piece of fine writing to catch the attention of their audience. All tales worth telling had been told many times; the only hope for the author to achieve fame was to make his own version more beautiful or more striking than the rest.

To do this, Rhetoric concentrated on three points: the organization of the story, the length, and the style. The stock advice on arrangement was not, in essence, very different from that given to the White Rabbit: ' "Begin at the beginning", the King said gravely, "and go on until you come to the end; then stop." ' There are, however, various methods of starting; for you can plunge in at the deep end and show the final situation before explaining how it arose; or, on the other hand, you can start with a *Sententia* (a proverb or cliché) and then elaborate it; or with an *Exemplum* (a similar case) and show the parallels between it and your main story.

Assuming that the audience's attention is now fully engaged, and has survived the transition to the main narrative (and this is not always done as subtly as it might be—witness Chaucer in *Troilus and Criseyde*: 'For now wol I gon streight to my matere'), the next problem is the Procrustean one of fitting the story to the space available. If it is too short it must be expanded; if it is too long, abbreviated. There are at least half a dozen ways of expanding your material; the principles upon which they work are two: the importation of extraneous matter, and the repetition of what you already have. One way of adding material is the use of stock passages, clichés or commonplaces. Terms like these are now felt to be derogatory, so it may be better to adapt the Latin technical term and call them *topics*. From the stocks provided by the manuals of rhetoric, an author could bring out *descriptions* of anything he fancied. The description of Blanche in the *Book of the Duchess* is very like the stock description in the *Nova Poetria* of Geoffroy de Vinsauf.

Another topic of a different sort is the poet's protestation of incapacity and reluctance to write. The Franklin, for instance, begins his Tale by disclaiming all knowledge of the rhetorical *figures*—then goes on to use them most skilfully. Another way is to use *digressions*, whether to another part of the story, or to something quite separate: a parallel example, for instance, or a proverb. Thus Chauntecleer in the *Nun's Priest's Tale* provides several examples of dreams that were proved to be true.

The second way is to expand a simple statement by repeating it in rather different terms. The first eighteen lines of the *Prologue* to the *Canterbury Tales* (quoted on p. 9) can be paraphrased as 'In spring people like to go on pilgrimages' but then, although the statement would be true enough, all the poetry would be lost; but rhetoric shows us how even this sort of bathos can be turned to good account, as when the Franklin laughs at his own rhetoric:

> . . . Til that the brighte sonne loste his hewe;
> For th' orisonte hath reft the sonne his lyght,—   *horizon*
> This is as muche to seye as it was nyght!—
>
> CT: FRANKLIN'S TALE V, 1016–18

There are other forms of repetition besides, where words and phrases are repeated either to link sections together, or more insistently so that they ring in the ear like a drum beat. The use of devices like this lies more in the emphasis of meaning than in the expansion of the story.

Writers seem to have felt less need to abbreviate their material. A previous version of a story, it was felt, was best improved by adding new adornment, not by cutting it short. True, there were occasions when it was necessary, and for these the figure called *occupatio*, or a refusal to tell what happened next, was prescribed. In the *Knight's Tale* Chaucer uses it to avoid describing Emelye's rites at the temple of Diana:

> But hou she dide her ryte I dare not telle.

Another passage in the *Knight's Tale* uses this device in quite another manner. At the end, when Arcite lies dead, Chaucer comes to deal with his funeral and starts with the pyre:

> But how the fyr was maked upon highte,
> Ne eek the names that the trees highte,   *were called*
> As ook, firre, birch, aspe, alder, holm, popler,   *aspen*   *holm oak*
> Wylugh, elm, plane, assh, box, chasteyn, lynde, laurer,   *willow*
> *chestnut*

> Mapul, thorn, bech, hasel, ew, whippeltree,— *cornel tree*
> How they weren feld, shal nat be toold for me. . . .
>
> CT: KNIGHT'S TALE I, 2919–24

This already seems a trifle long-winded for a conventional *occupatio*, but more is to come. He describes the whole proceedings, saying all the while that this is what he is not going to do, and in the end the passage extends to fifty lines. Here he is not using the device to cut a long story short, but to keep his audience with him, by appearing unwilling to describe the scene; human nature being what it is, this makes us all want to know more, and consequently we hang upon his words. This device exerts the same sort of fascination as a seaside 'What the butler saw' machine.

It also goes to show that a creative writer can always turn the manuals of instruction to his own use. Molière's M. Jourdain was amazed to learn that he spoke prose; Wordsworth, no doubt, would have been equally amazed if he had been told that he was using *dubitatio*, one of the several kinds of apostrophe, when he wrote:

> O Cuckoo, shall I call thee Bird,
> Or but a wandering voice?

Chaucer, on the other hand, could not have failed to be aware of what the rhetoricians taught; but to what extent he used them consciously, or relied on his own ability as a writer, is a vexed and fruitless question. It is possible to go through his poems against a manual of rhetoric and spend hours picking out examples of the figures, but even then we cannot be certain that their use is a result of the direct influence of the manuals; he may well have used that particular figure in that particular place because it was the natural way of expressing what he wanted to say. Besides, the manuals are primarily analytical; that is, they take what previous writers have done and analyse and codify the means by which they produce their effects. When it comes to reversing the process and using them to compose a poem, something more is needed, and that is ability to write: those who already have that will not have much need of what the manuals tell them.

And yet it would be wrong to think that they are entirely without value; on the broader issues of arrangement, and some aspects of amplification, particularly by juxtaposition of parallel examples, they are useful even now. Smaller questions of style, especially the enumeration of all the figures of thought, are of lesser poetic importance, and I will not consider them here, except to mention one important preliminary question of style. This is the doctrine of the three styles, for it is wrong to talk of style without qualification. There are in fact three styles, the high, middle and low styles, varying in elaboration with the importance of the subject. This is one of the jokes in the *Nun's Priest's Tale*, that Chaucer uses the high style, fit for only the most important and tragic subjects, to tell a story about domestic fowls in a farmyard.

We can see the teaching of the rhetoricians in the structure and movement of the *Parlement of Foules*: this poem is particularly satisfying when we see what Chaucer was trying to do, but singularly lacking in balance to the untutored modern reader. However, an analysis of the poem long enough to do it justice would be too long for this chapter, and accordingly it is deferred until Chapter 6.

5

Chaucer's Language and Verse

So far I have tried to clear away some of the intellectual difficulties that stand in the way of an understanding of what Chaucer wrote 600 years ago. However, the resolution of these difficulties is not worth a great deal if the two more technical difficulties presented by the forms of his language and his verse remain. There is little virtue in being able to explain Chaucer's world picture, and yet not to be able to construe his words.

The difficulty to a modern reader of Chaucer's English arises from the way in which all languages are constantly changing. When we consider how little of a modern conversation would have been fully understood by, say, Tennyson, only a hundred years ago, and when we consider that Tennyson is now being extensively annotated by scholars (though it is easier for us to understand him than he us) we can appreciate Chaucer's remarks on this very problem:

> Ye knowe ek that in forme of speche is chaunge
> Withinne a thousand yeer, and wordes tho   *then*
> That hadden pris, now wonder nyce and straunge
> Us thinketh hem, and yet thei spake hem so
> And spedde as wel in love as men now do. . . .

TROILUS AND CRISEYDE II, 22–6

Observe also that this passage illustrates some of the difficulties produced by changes in the language. There are obsolete words (*ek*, also, and *tho*, then); obsolete syntax—*us thinketh* is not just bad grammar for 'we think'; it is an impersonal construction—'it seems to us'—which is a survival from an earlier period of the language; and, most important and most difficult of all, there are words which are still recognizable, but whose meanings have changed completely in the past six centuries: *nice* is one of the most notorious examples of this in English. Ultimately it derives from the Latin *nescio* ('I am ignorant of') by way of French, but down through the centuries its meaning has gradually changed through 'unknown', 'strange' (its meaning in this passage), 'rare', 'tender', 'delicate', 'fastidious', 'precise', 'refined', 'cultured', 'agreeable', and finally to its indefinable modern usage in which we apply it to anything we vaguely approve off, from a nice girl to a nice dinner.

These changes since Chaucer's time have occurred in the first two-thirds of his 'thousand yeer', but the history of English stretches back as far beyond Chaucer as he is distant from us. His language is only one stage of continuous development, and because he happened to live at one of the more important periods of this development, it will probably help if I briefly sketch in the history of our language from Old English, through Middle English to the beginnings of the language we speak today.

OLD ENGLISH

Old English, as the term implies, is the oldest period in the history of the language; it extended until about a century after the Norman Conquest. Middle English continued until the end of the 15th century; from then on is what we call Modern English. (The reader will realize, of course, that these three terms are created by scholars for the purposes of analysis and discussion, and will not think that they imply that sudden changes took place in 1166 or 1499, but merely that it is convenient to talk of the English of King Alfred's time as Old English, and that this is manifestly different in certain definable and obvious ways from the Middle English of Chaucer and his contemporaries.)

The beginnings lie back in the 5th and 6th centuries A.D. when Britain was invaded by a group of related Germanic tribes. Bede, the first English historian, writing of course in Latin, at the beginning of the 8th century, says that the invaders were three of the most formidable tribes of Germans: the Angles, the Saxons and the Jutes. The Jutes settled in Kent and the Isle of Wight, the Saxons in the rest of the south and south-west, and the Angles in the Midlands and the north of England. The Jutes have gone unremembered; but the Angles and the Saxons gave their name to Anglo-Saxon, the now old-fashioned name for Old English, as well as to East Anglia, and to Sussex, Essex and Middlesex, the lands of the South, East and Middle Saxons. The Angles settled much more of the country than East Anglia: they split into two groups, those north of the Humber, or Northumbrians, and those who settled on the borders, or *marches*, of Wales—the Mercians. These groups naturally differed somewhat in their speech, and from these differences spring the various dialects of today; but they had enough in common to form a new branch, English (Anglish), of the Germanic family of languages, as they developed in isolation from their cousins on the Continent.

The next invaders also spoke a related Germanic language; starting in the closing years of the 8th century and continuing in the 9th century, there were several waves of Scandinavian adventurers who came first merely to plunder, but later stayed to settle. Those from Norway gravitated to the north and west; those from Denmark to the south and east. The Norsemen sailed round the north of Scotland, taking in the Isles on the way (Orkney and Shetland were not finally ceded to the Scottish Crown until 1472), and settled in Ireland, the Isle of Man, and parts of the north-west of England, with, for a time, an offshoot to the east in the splendid but short-lived Norse kingdom of York. Yorkshire, the East Midlands and East Anglia were the province of the Danes, who kept up their own laws, language and customs, so that this area became known as the *Danelaw*. Their effect on the English language does not show itself till after the Norman Conquest, when the way in which Scandinavian words were adopted argues for a mingling of the two peoples. The author of the Icelandic *Saga of Gunnlaug Wormtongue* goes further:

> In those days they used the same language in England as in Norway and Denmark, but there came a change of tongue in England once William the Bastard conquered it, and from then on French was the language of England, because he, William, was of French descent.   SAGA OF GUNNLAUG WORMTONGUE 7

This is a rather more detached view of the Norman Conquest than our own, which is coloured by our descent also from the invaders, so that we tend to forget that in 1066 an alien way of life was imposed from above by foreigners speaking an entirely different language—for French is one of the group of languages directly descended from Latin, while the Germanic family of languages certainly is not.

Because, unlike the Danes and Norsemen, the Normans had control of the central government, introduced their own aristocracy, and occupied all the positions of high office, French displaced English as the language of government, just as English was to be used throughout the British Empire and is still used even when British rule has ceased and in cases where all other connection with Britain is severed.

English was of course still spoken by the bulk of the population; the racial distinction between the use of English and French must soon have turned into a social one, for the upper classes governed in French while everybody else went about their business in English. There is evidence, too, that French was used officially for long after it had ceased to be the native tongue of the nobility, and that by the 14th century those who could speak French were certainly bilingual. The first Royal Proclamation to be issued in English as well as French dates from 1258, though this is an isolated example and there were political reasons for wanting the largest possible audience for it. Another century was to pass before English received official recognition. In 1362 the *Statute of Pleading* was enacted to ensure that proceedings at law should now be heard in English, because 'French is much unknown in the said realm'. When Richard II was deposed in the year before Chaucer's death, the languages used were Latin and English, and the order of deposition and Henry IV's claim to the throne were delivered in English. By way of contrast, the foundation statutes of The Queen's College, Oxford, of 1340 (a few years before Chaucer's birth) require the use of only Latin and French in the college. It would seem that even then Oxford was the home of lost causes!

MIDDLE ENGLISH

The English that once more came into official use was by now quite different from that which was spoken before the Norman Conquest. Old English is an inflected language, like Latin, in which the relationship between the words in a sentence is shown by their form. Middle English, the new official language, is more like modern German; it has lost most of the inflections and in consequence is much more dependent upon prepositions and word order to show the construction of the sentence. In one way this makes it easier for us to read a Middle English author like Chaucer, because the general pattern of his sentences is like our own; but in another way we can be caught out by survivals of older forms which we may not expect because externally they look just like our own modern ones. Take, for example, 'his hors were goode', in the description of the Knight from the *General Prologue*. *Hors* appears to us to be singular—it is not until we reach *were* that we realize it must be plural; and in less obvious examples we can be badly led astray. Another case of a noun, which, for historical linguistic reasons, is uninflected where we would expect an inflection in modern English, is *lady* in the phrase from the description of the Squire: 'to stonden in his lady grace'. This uninflected genitive, common to feminine nouns in Old English, survives today only in set phrases like *Lady Day*; elsewhere the feminine nouns of Modern English have adopted the *'s* for the genitive by analogy with the masculine nouns.

Secondly, Middle English acquired a vast number of foreign words, particularly from the French- and Scandinavian-speaking invaders. The borrowings from the French reflect, to a considerable degree, the social position of the French. The language of government, law, military affairs and the Church depends heavily on French words. A short list may show this: *Parliament, government, crown, empire, sovereign, statute, tax, exchequer, chancellor, treasurer*, are all French in origin, and so too are all titles of rank apart from the native *king, queen, lord, lady* and *earl*; this reflects, no doubt, the decimation of the English nobility at the time of the Conquest. In law, *justice, crime, judgement, plaintiff, defendant, bail, bar, assize, verdict*, are all French. And, turning to more domestic matters, it is pleasant to speculate, as did Sir Walter Scott in *Ivanhoe*, that the modern words for dead meat, ready for consumption, come from the French, while the words for the live animals are all English, because it was the French-speakers who would be able to eat meat more often and who saw it on the table instead of on the hoof. At any rate, we still have the pairs *cow/beef*; *sheep/mutton*; *pig/pork*; *calf/veal*; *deer/venison*.

The influx of French words is the biggest and most obvious single difference between Old and Middle English vocabulary; but there was also extensive borrowing of Scandinavian words, brought by the Norse and Danish invaders. Their language and Old English were similar, and moreover there was not the same social difference between them and the Anglo-Saxons. In consequence, a Scandinavian form has sometimes replaced the English word from the same root: an extreme example is the singular *he*, *him*, *his*, which are English, side by side with the plural *they*, *them*, *their*, which are Scandinavian. (*'em* is not really an illiterate form of *them*, in such phrases as 'Give 'em to me', but the descendant of the native English form *hem*.) Similarly, Scandinavian *taka* gradually replaced the Old English *niman*, so that by the 16th century *nim* had become merely a slang expression, and *take* was the word in normal use; in Shakespeare's Corporal Nym—'sworn brother', with Bardolph, 'to filching'— the word still survives, but we miss the joke today.

Thirdly, the relative importance of the dialects had changed. By the end of the Old English period, West Saxon, the dialect of King Alfred's capital, Winchester, had become the standard literary language. After the Conquest, when for a time English was restricted to the uneducated, there was no longer such a thing as Standard English. Gradually, however, from the 14th century onwards the East Midlands dialect of London asserted itself, and became the ancestor of the Standard English of today. It had the great advantage of being the dialect of the seat of government, of the most populous area of the county, and of the two universities, Oxford and Cambridge; and finally, it had the prestige of the works of Chaucer and his contemporaries.

These are the sort of difficulties which were met by Caxton, as he explains in the prologue to his translation of the *Aeneid* of Virgil, which dates from 1490. The Abbot of Westminster had asked him to translate a work from Old English, but as he says: 'And certaynly it was wreton in suche wyse that it was more lyke to dutche (German, *deutsch*) than englysshe', so that he could not modernize it. Even during his own lifetime English had changed, for Englishmen are 'bourne under the dominacyoun of the mone'. Moreover, English spoken in one county, he says, is different from that of its neighbour. Take the example of a northern merchant called Sheffield, who set sail from London, and, putting in at the Foreland:

> . . . cam in to an hows and axed for mete, and specyally he axed after eggys. And the good wyf answerde, that she could speke no frensshe, but the marchaunt was angry, for he also coude speke no frensshe, but wolde haue hadde eggys, and she vnderstode hym not. And thenne at laste a nother sayd that he wolde haue eyren, then the good wyf sayd that she vnderstode hym wel. Loo what sholde a man in thyse dayes now wryte, eggys or eyren, certaynly it is harde to playse euery man, bycause of dyversyte and chaunge of langage.   PROLOGUES AND EPILOGUES, Caxton*

Caxton's merchant nearly went hungry, and if we had to speak or write Chaucer's English we might fare no better. Fortunately, it is far easier to read a language than to speak it. To get pleasure from reading Chaucer, it is not necessary to know Middle English grammar in detail; this short sketch of the language before Chaucer is intended merely to give the reader enough background to enable him to put Chaucer's English into perspective.

One thing to watch for, however, is the way in which many words have so changed in meaning since Chaucer's day while keeping much the same form: *nice* has already been instanced; *humour* is another outstanding one. The beginner must look up all words in the glossary at first, just in case they have changed in meaning. After a time he will learn the old meanings, and Chaucer will have on him something of the effect he intended 600 years ago.

Those who want to make a study of Middle English will be well served by a Grammar which deals with the whole of the language. The two main ones in English are the *Elementary*

---

* E.E.T.S. OS.176, 108.

Middle English Grammar by Joseph and Elizabeth Mary Wright, and the *Handbook of Middle English* by Mossé, which is translated from the French. Of these, Mossé has the advantage of giving a wide selection of texts.

PRONUNCIATION

Chaucer's works were originally read aloud to an audience, not silently by individuals. A manuscript of *Troilus and Criseyde* in Trinity College, Cambridge, has as a frontispiece a picture of Chaucer reading to the Court. If we can learn to read him in an approximation to the original sound, much of his artistry will come clearer, and at the same time the meaning of many words which has been obscured by the spelling will be revealed by the relationship of the pronunciation to the modern sound. A rough and ready rule is to pronounce words of French origin as if they were French, and words of native or Germanic origin as if they were German. This works because the pronunciation of long vowels has, since Chaucer's day, changed far more in English than in continental languages.

In some cases, a few minutes of oral instruction are worth pages of print; this is one of them, and fortunately there are several records now of modern scholars reading Chaucer in what we think is the original pronunciation. The first of these (ARGO, RG 401) contains the *Prologue* to the *Canterbury Tales* read by three Oxford scholars: Nevill Coghill, Norman Davis and John Burrow. Listen to this if you possibly can and see how the text comes alive.

A more detailed treatment than can be found in most editions of the texts is the thin pamphlet *A Guide to Chaucer's Pronunciation* by Helge Kökeritz.

VERSIFICATION

Assuming that we now can cope generally with the pronunciation of Chaucer, we can begin to read his verse aloud for ourselves. But we soon come up against a new snag: it doesn't appear to scan.

There may be said to be two reasons for this. First, French words like *honour* require the accent to be put where it still is in modern French, on the second syllable: *honoúr*, *coráge*. We soon get used to this. But the second reason is more elusive.

Final -e

One of the trickiest problems in Chaucer pronunciation is that presented by the final -e, found at the end of many words. At the beginning of the 14th century these were generally sounded as separate syllables, but by the end of that century they had become silent, at any rate in common speech. Verse tends to retain the old-fashioned usages; final -e is still pronounced, or at least scanned, in French verse, centuries after it became silent in prose; and people's habits of speech do not change much as they grow older—which is why old people tend to sound old-fashioned and to criticize the speech-habits of their grandchildren which fore-shadow what will become standard usage in another fifty years. On both these counts it looks as if we ought to pronounce the final -e except perhaps where it can be elided before a following vowel or silent h. Unfortunately, we cannot check this assump-tion by trying to scan Chaucer's verse, because theories about his versification have been derived from presuppositions about his use of final -e. We are caught, in fact, in a circular argument.

COMMON ENGLISH RHYTHM

From the 16th to the 19th centuries, as one of the greatest technicians in verse said, English verse has been:

> measured by feet of either two or three syllables and (putting aside the imperfect feet at the beginning and end of lines and also some unusual measures, in which feet seem to be paired together and double or composite feet arise) never more nor less.
>
> Every foot has one principal stress or accent, and this or the syllable it falls on may be called the Stress of the foot and the other part, the one or two unaccented syllables, the Slack. Feet (and the rhythms made out of them) in which the Stress comes first are called Falling Feet and Falling Rhythms, feet and rhythm in which the Slack comes first are called Rising Feet and Rhythms, and if the Stress is between two Slacks there will be Rocking Feet and Rhythms.   GERARD MANLEY HOPKINS, *Penguin ed.* p. 7

But to prevent this basic rhythm from becoming monotonous, poets have always 'brought in licences and departures from the rule to give variety'. It is this 'Common English Rhythm', as Hopkins calls it, that unites the 18th-century heroic couplet and

Shakespeare in a single tradition, though the sturdiness of Shakespeare's blank verse is a far cry from the polish of Pope's, evident even when he himself reverses a foot:

Slight is the subject, but not so the praise

If She inspire and He approve my lays.

RAPE OF THE LOCK 5-6

Chaucer's verse, too, has usually been interpreted in the light of this tradition, so that the longer lines of his later work are read as five-stressed decasyllabic lines, and the shorter lines of his earlier work as four-stressed octosyllabic. In each case the rhythm is rising—or iambic, to adopt the classical terminology. To ensure that Chaucer's verse fits this pattern, he is allowed by way of licence to have an extra unstressed syllable at the mid-line pause, or caesura, and at the end of the line, and to omit an unstressed initial syllable—that is, to have only nine syllables in some lines. Unaccented final -e must then be everywhere pronounced, except when it is followed by a vowel, a silent *h* in words from the French (e.g. *honour*), or certain unimportant almost auxiliary words which have a lightly sounded *h* (e.g. *he*, *her*, *him*, *hem*, *hadde*). Read on these assumptions, the first lines of the *Prologue* would go something like this: (N.B. unsounded final -e's are enclosed in parentheses):

Whan that Aprill with his shoures soote   (initial syllable omitted)

The droght(e) of March hath perced to the roote,   (*to* stressed)

And bathed every veyn(e) in swich licour

Of which vertu engendred is the flour;   (*is* stressed)

Whan Zephyrus eek with his sweete breeth   (*with* stressed)

Inspired hath in every holt and heeth

The tendre croppes, and the yonge sonne   (*and* stressed)

Hath in the Ram his halve cours yronne,   (reversed first foot)

And smale foweles maken melodye,　　　　(extra syllable at caesura)
That slepen al the nyght with open ye
(So priketh hem Natur(e) in hir corages):　　　(*hem, hir* stressed)
Thann(e) longen folk to goon on pilgrimages,
And palmeres for to seken straunge strondes　　(*for* stressed)
To ferne halwes, kowth(e) in sondry londes;

Now theories of English grammar have, until comparatively recently, treated the language as if it were classical Latin. (We saw in Chapter 4 (pp. 76–9) how Grammar in schools and universities was simply Latin grammar, and how this continued past the Renaissance.) The same is true of versification, though here too the characters of the languages are quite different. Classical Latin verse consists of a pattern of long and short syllables arranged in a limited number of feet. A certain amount of substitution is permitted to prevent monotony, so that the number of syllables in a line may vary, though the number of feet is fixed. After the classical period, Latin verse introduced rhyme and became accentual not quantitative; that is, it was based on stress, not length of syllable. This is the origin, not only of 'Common English Rhythm', but also of French and other modern European verse forms, which depend on a fixed number of syllables and pattern of stress.

OLD ENGLISH VERSE

In view of this common origin there would have been no question about the sort of verse Chaucer wrote, were it not that Old English verse was constructed on very different principles, and this verse-form survived into Chaucer's lifetime. The Old English line was divided into two half-lines; each of these had two stressed syllables, and any convenient number of unstressed syllables, with, in some cases, a third lighter stress as well. There was no intentional rhyme; instead, there was an elaborate alliterative structure wherein one of the stresses in the first half of the line must begin with the same letter as the first stress of the second half. Both the stresses of the first half may alliterate; the final stress rarely can. Though alliterative verse like this survived the Norman Conquest, and several major 14th-century poems use it, it died out not much later under the influence of continental models and the new interest in the classics characteristic of the Renaissance; it was revived, though without the same kind of alliteration, by Hopkins in his 'Sprung Rhythm'. (Hopkins did, of course, employ very elaborate alliteration, but not on the Old English model, as a rule.)

The following passage from Langland's *Piers Plowman* may serve as an example of 14th-century alliterative verse: it is an almost exact contemporary of the *Canterbury Tales*.

> In a somer sesoun. whan soft was the sonne,
> I shope me in shroudes . as I a shepe were,
> In habite as an heremite . unholy of workes
> Went wyde in this world . wondres to here.
> Ac on a May mornynge . on Malverne hulles
> Me byfel a ferly . of fairy me thoughte;
> I was wery forwandred . and went me to reste
> Under a brode banke . bi a bornes side,
> And as I lay and lened . and loked in the wateres,
> I slombered in a slepyng . it sweyved so merye.

PIERS PLOWMAN B text, Prologue 1–10

Now a recent attempt has been made to prove that Chaucer was in fact following this tradition in his verse, rather than the continental rhyming tradition of fixed numbers of syllables. J. G. Southworth, in *Verses of Cadence*, scans the opening lines of the *Prologue* somewhat like this:

> Whan that Aprill with his shoures soote
> The droghte of March hath perced to the roote

95

And bathed every veyne in swich licour
Of which vertu engendred is the flour
Whan Zephyrus eek with his sweete breeth
Inspired hath in every holt and heeth
The tendre croppes, and the yonge sonne
Hath in the Ram his half cours yronne
And smale foweles maken melodye
That slepen al the nyght with open ye
(So priketh hem Nature in hir corages)
Thanne longen folk to goon on pilgrimages
And palmeres for to seken straunge strondes
To ferne halwes kowthe in sondry londes

The main difference between the two interpretations of this passage derives from the pronunciation or not of the final unstressed -e.

We do not know for certain whether Chaucer's contemporaries scanned it in the verse or not; we do think, however, that they did not pronounce it in normal speech.

Southworth's contention is that all modern texts are edited on the assumption that the final -e was pronounced according to the rules given on page 93. A study of the manuscripts, he says, would support his opinion that the final -e was not scanned and that the verse is alliterative, not quantitative: native, that is, not continental. Since no extant manuscript is in Chaucer's hand, and they are all written in the 15th century anyhow, there seems no likelihood of a definite solution as yet. Still, we can get the flavour of Chaucer's verse pretty well if we read him in the traditional way, remembering as we do it that behind the conventional iambic or rising rhythm there may be the older pattern of alliterative stressed verse, forming as it were a counterpoint.

6

Chaucer's Works: The Early Poems

Chaucer's reputation today depends mainly upon the *Canterbury Tales*; but in bulk they form rather less than half of those works of his which have come down to us. Besides a number of shorter poems, there are five or six other major works in verse and two or three in prose. With these last I shall not attempt to deal. They are a translation of the *De Consolatione Philosophiae* of Boethius and the *Treatise on the Astrolabe*, both of which are accepted as genuine; and another scientific treatise, the *Equatorie of the Planets*, dating from the year 1392 (one year after the *Astrolabe* treatise). This latter work was discovered after the Second World War in the library of Peterhouse, Cambridge, by Dr. D. J. Price, who has attributed it to Chaucer; no incontrovertible evidence has appeared either to prove or disprove this, so the question is still open.

These two astronomical works belong rather to the history of science than to literary criticism. True, we would understand the contemporary mind better if we read and digested them, but I hope that the résumé of scientific ideas given in Chapter 3 will be enough for the purposes of the ordinary reader. Similarly with the philosophical work, the translation of Boethius, one of the formative writers of the Middle Ages. Chaucer was not the only person to translate it into English before changing fashions in education put it out of favour; he was preceded by King Alfred the Great and succeeded by Queen Elizabeth the First. Its interest nowadays lies, for scholars, in the influence it had on other writers and on Chaucer's own works. Anyone who wants to read Boethius for his own sake would be better served by a modern translation.

Gc

Scholars at one time divided Chaucer's works into three 'periods': the French, Italian and English periods. To the first belong his translation of the *Romance of the Rose*, the *Book of the Duchess*, and a minor poem, the *ABC*, a translation of a French poem in honour of the Blessed Virgin Mary which, according to Speght's edition of Chaucer (1598), was made 'at the request of Blanch, Duchesse of Lancaster, as a praier for her privat vse, being a woman in her religion very deuout'. Blanche is, of course, the Duchess commemorated in the *Book*: she was John of Gaunt's first wife (his third, we remember, was Chaucer's own sister-in-law, see p. 16) who died of the plague on 12 September 1369.

Up to this point in his career Chaucer is said to have followed the French tradition in which he was schooled. But in 1372 he visited Italy for the first time, and it is considered likely that works which show a close acquaintance with Italian authors must have been written after this visit: hence the Italian 'period'. To this belong the *Legend of Good Women*, the *House of Fame*, the *Parlement of Foules* and *Troilus and Criseyde*, as well as early versions of the *Knight's Tale* and the *Second Nun's Tale*. These must have been written by 1386, since Chaucer mentions them all in the *Legend of Good Women*, the earliest version of which is known to be not later than this.

The English 'period' is dated from the time Chaucer resigned from the Customs. To this time belongs the composition of the *Canterbury Tales* as a whole, though, as we have seen, certain of the tales were written before this and incorporated into the grand scheme.

Whether these 'periods' have any validity is a perennial question among the scholars, and not only in regard to Chaucer. It is a fascinating question, bringing in many considerations of greater and lesser importance. For instance, how far is Chaucer an original writer? Many of his works are mere translations, while others are clearly based quite closely on borrowed stories—in fact, the only Canterbury Tales that are not traceable to other writers are the earthy yarns of such characters as the Miller, and these are probably the sort passed round among the people.

But Chaucer lived in a time when writers worked on the assumption that all tales worth telling had been told long ago, and all a man could do was write a variation on an old theme—give it a new twist. In a way, I suppose, this is true: there are said to be only five basic jokes in the comic postcard market; and themes from the Greek tragedies still recur today: T. S. Eliot's *Family Reunion* and Anouilh's *Antigone* are only two cases out of many.

Again, Chaucer's aim was to make English literature acceptable in Court circles. Whether this was a conscious aim or not, he had no choice but to start where he did. He was brought up at Court, at a Court moreover where French was the language of culture and where the audiences expected something like the *Romance*. If he had produced the *Prologue* to the *Canterbury Tales* to this audience at this time he would not have got a hearing. However, his lifetime fell during the period when the English language was being emancipated; we have seen how English came to be used in the Courts of Law, in Parliament and in the schools; by the end of the century it was acceptable in literature for the Court. Remember how Gower received the royal command (p. 73); and the book which resulted from it, the *Confessio Amantis*, was, despite its Latin title, written in English. If a writer wants to win his contemporaries' ears, he cannot afford to be too far ahead of his time. This is why Chaucer started from the French, but it was only a start; throughout his life, whatever his sources, his treatment of them is entirely his own. It is true that at first he seems to be using French models, and that there is a group of works in which the influence of Italian writers predominated, but he is using other sources as well. And, indeed, to call his last 'period' his English one seems to be taking refuge in the mongrel nature of the English nation itself. The foreign influences are still there; even in his verse (unless we accept the theories of J. G. Southworth (p. 96)) he does not use the traditional English form which some of his contemporaries, such as Langland, used—the old alliterative verse of *Piers Plowman*.

THE POEMS

In this chapter I propose to deal only with representative poems from the first two of these three periods: the *Romance of the Rose* and the *Parlement of Foules*. Of the rest, the *Book of the Duchess*, though complete, is very immature; the *House of Fame* is interesting only for the autobiographical fragments and for the clear change of style from Book I, which is like the *Book of the Duchess*, to Book II, which foreshadows the developments to be found in the *Parlement of Foules*; moreover, it is unfinished and so fails to provide the satisfaction to be gained from a whole work—though the eagle in Book II is amusing as a sort of schoolmasterly guide. The *Legend of Good Women* likewise is unfinished. Here the most interesting part is the prologue in conventional praise of the daisy. The body of the work is a series of stories about women who faithfully served the God of Love; as a collection it looks forward to the *Canterbury Tales*, but the stories are boring by comparison, so that it is no wonder that Chaucer never finished them. After all, who wants to hear about *good* women?

THE 'ROMANCE OF THE ROSE'

Any account of Chaucer's early poetry must begin with the *Romance of the Rose*, a translation of a famous French allegorical love poem, the source of inspiration for many poets who came after. Chaucer tells it as a dream in which the dreamer woos his lady: but it is told allegorically, that is, the changing psychological states of the dreamer and the lady are shown not by soliloquies which might break the flow of the action too much, nor by plain description, nor by a 'stream-of-consciousness' which might well obscure the action altogether, but by introducing figures which personify the emotion of the actors in the story. Thus the interplay of all the emotions that may be acting upon one person at any one time is shown by argument, or fights, between the personifications. An imaginary example may help. Suppose a little boy is hesitating before taking a shilling from his mother's purse to buy himself a bar of chocolate; he knows he ought not, and is half afraid to, but he wants the chocolate so badly that his greed gets the better of him. This could be shown allegorically by describing an argument between Fear and Conscience on the one hand and Greed on the other, in which Greed finally wins. This convention is strange to modern ears, but then we have been conditioned (and my use of this word proves it) to think of the workings of the mind in quite another way. And this means that whatever gains may have come from the theories of Freud and Jung, in terms of literature we have lost the advantage of being able to suggest the nature of these emotional forces by the images the author gives for them.

So far I have spoken as if the *Romance of the Rose* were a single poem; in fact, it is in two halves. It was begun about 1237 by Guillaume de Lorris, who wrote the first four and a half thousand lines; forty years later another poet, Jean de Meun, completed it at far greater length and in a very different style. The first part is the more important, as this is the part of the translation that is most probably by Chaucer. In it the dreamer dreams that one May morning he is walking beside a river, when he comes to a walled garden, into which at last he manages to gain entrance through a small wicket gate. It is the garden of Delight, who is taking his pleasure there with all his followers. The garden represents the courtly life; this is made more explicit in the poem by the description of the paintings round the outside of the wall which depict the qualities which would debar anyone from entering. The action so far shows the young man's entry to society; next, he falls in love, and this is shown by his being wounded to the heart by Cupid's arrows as he is gazing into a pair of crystal stones in a well—his lady's eyes—reflected in which he sees a rosebud, as yet unopened, in a thorn-hedged rosegarden. The bud symbolizes her love. In fact, the lady never appears in person; we see her only through the personification of certain traits of her character; but she is no less real for all that, and an essentially static story gains a dynamic interest by this means. The rest of this part of the poem shows her reactions to the dreamer's advances, through the struggle between Belacoil (Fair Welcome), Pity and Fraunchise (Nobility) on the one hand, and Daunger (Rebuff), Fear and Shame (Modesty) on the other. There is no need to tell any more of the story; the points to watch out for, because they crop up again and again, are the dream, the garden, and the personifications.

The *Romance of the Rose* is entirely French in conception and presentation. It assumes in its readers a familiarity with courtly life, and above all an acquiescence in the code of Courtly Love, an acquiescence in which Chaucer himself obviously shares. But it is a translation, not an adaptation, so we cannot read Chaucer's true feelings from it. It is therefore most refreshing to pass from this to the *Parlement of Foules*, in which we can see unmistakably the imprint of the individual Chaucer, whose sceptical mind shows itself here for the first time. For instance, the very first line makes its effect by showing us a familiar thing in a strange context: it is one of Hippocrates' maxims, and had always been applied, naturally, to medicine, as Chaucer's readers would well know; it is not until the fourth line that we realize, with a bit of a shock, that the whole poem is, though in the form of a 'love-vision', basically an ironical comment on the very strange phenomenon called *Courtly Love*, or *Amour Courtois*. This we must briefly examine before we pass on to the poem itself.

COURTLY LOVE

Courtly Love is a phenomenon which sprang up in Provence at the end of the 11th century. It is important because it formed the subject of the entertainment provided at the Royal Courts of France and England for several centuries, and in particular it was the subject of the poems by Guillaume de Machaut, Eustace Deschamps and above all the *Romance of the Rose*, all of which were known at the English Court and which Chaucer knew and used so much. As the name implies, its practice was restricted to the nobility, or at least the knightly class and those above who formed the Royal Court. In fact it was laid down that the bourgeoisie and the villein class were insufficiently refined to understand and appreciate its rules.

These rules at their most elaborate constituted for the courtly lover almost another state within the state, with its own religion, army and courts of law. According to these rules the relation between the lover and his lady is very much the same as between a feudal vassal and his lord. He serves her without necessarily expecting any reward, no matter what her whims may be, and receives all her rebukes and cruelty in silence, no matter how undeserved. He is her man in the feudal sense, and the early Provençal poems make this clear, for in them the lady is addressed as *mi dons*, my lord. This being so, Courtly Love is obviously incompatible with marriage, for in marriage the woman should be subject to the man. So in the early stages, the woman whom a poet celebrates is almost certainly the wife of another, and because their love is clandestine and yet widely accepted as the done thing, his rival is not her husband (who presumably is attached to somebody else's wife) but other lovers. In this complicated situation he is only saved from despair by his faith in the God of Love. And just as the service of love was an image of feudal service, so that lovers were said to be serving in Love's army, so too there was a religion of Love which employed the images of the Church. It was not always taken as far as the Latin poem of the time, which parodies the practices of the Church, where the God of Love sends his Cardinal to examine a convent of nuns, and to excommunicate heretics who are led to confess after a service in which Ovid, poet of the Art of Love, is read instead of the Gospel. It would be wrong to treat this poem as typical or to build too much upon it; nevertheless, in one of the Arthurian romances by Chrétien de Troyes, Lancelot genuflects on leaving Guinevere's room, as if it were a church.

A third part of the system is the Courts of Love, at which questions of correct behaviour were settled and punishment meted out to those lovers whose conduct did not measure up to the elaborate rules. At such a court the following case was tried:

> Two men who were in all things absolutely equal began to pay court at the same time and in the same manner and demanded urgently that they be loved. Therefore it was asked which man's love could be chosen in such a case. We are taught by the admonition of the same countess that in such a case the man who asks first should be given the preference; but if their proposals seem to be simultaneous, it is not unfair to leave it to the woman to choose the one to whom she finds her heart inclining.
>
> THE ART OF COURTLY LOVE, Andreas Capellanus*

* Trans. J. J. Parry, 169.

This is handed down as the decision of the Countess of Champagne, whose chaplain Andreas was at the end of the 12th century. The whole proceeding has a flavour of the lawyers' moot about it, or Marie Antoinette and the French Court playing at milkmaids at Versailles. And this may raise the question of how seriously Courtly Love was taken. From the sociologist's point of view this is an important question, but for the critic of literature it is largely irrelevant; the code of Courtly Love shows clearly in the poems and stories written for the entertainment of the Court, and so must be taken into account when we are reading that literature, whether or not the audience actually practised what they heard. In fact it would be quite possible to argue that what gave literature its piquancy was the fact that it showed a society which was the mirror image of their own, but was organized upon quite different premises.

So far I have been discussing Courtly Love in its original form with its four distinctive marks as described by C. S. Lewis: 'Humility, Courtesy, Adultery, and the Religion of Love'. These no longer hold good for the English romances of the 14th century in which what begins as Courtly Love, or at least is described in its terms, ends up as marriage. It shows, I think, that Courtly Love was very much a thing of the Court and that outside it, especially as literacy spread amongst the middle classes, stories would naturally reflect the ways of thought of their audience, just as the stories in women's magazines do today. It is true that many of these romances which do not subscribe to the tenets of Courtly Love have their origins in the provinces, away from the Court in London. But some of the *Canterbury Tales* themselves are in the same vein; in the *Knight's Tale*, what started as worship at a distance ends in marriage:

> And thus with alle blisse and melodye
> Hath Palamon ywedded Emelye . . .
> . . . And Emelye hym loveth so tendrely,
> And he hire serveth al so gentilly. . . .

CT: KNIGHT'S TALE I, 3097–103

The opening of the *Franklin's Tale* shows how the two traditions can be reconciled by mutual respect between husband and wife:

> . . . Ther was a knyght that loved and dide his payne   *took pains*
> To serve a lady in his beste wise;   *as best he could*
> And many a labour, many a greet emprise   *enterprise*
> He for his lady wroghte, er she were wonne.
> For she was oon the faireste under sonne,
> And eek therto comen of so heigh kynrede   *lineage*
> That wel unnethes dorste this knyght, for drede,   *scarcely*
> Telle hire his wo, his peyne, and his distresse.
> But atte laste she, for his worthynesse,
> And namely for his meke obeysaunce,   *humble attention*
> Hath swich a pitee caught of his penaunce   *suffering*
> That pryvely she fil of his accord   *secretly*
> To take hym for hir housbonde and hir lord. . . .
>
> CT: FRANKLIN'S TALE V, 730–42

That, apart from the one word *housbonde*, is the position of the courtly lover in a nutshell. He has served her faithfully, suffering the pains of love for her sake until his worth and obedient submission moved her to pity. When she has given him her hand, he swears never to act as her master and force her against her will; that is, he forswears his rights as husband and she forswears her rights in the Courtly Love code by promising to be his 'humble trewe wyf', and thus:

> Heere may man seen an humble, wys accord;
> Thus hath she take hir servant and hir lord,—
> Servant in love, and lord in mariage.
> Thanne was he bothe in lordshipe and servage.
> Servage? nay, but in lordshipe above,
> Sith he hath bothe his lady and his love;
> His lady, certes, and his wyf also,
> The which that lawe of love acordeth to.
>
> CT: FRANKLIN'S TALE V, 791–8

Courtly Love, in fact, cannot have been practised in the last resort, any more than Marie Antoinette, Queen of France, can have become a milkmaid: cows have to be milked and mucked out, and children (so society says) have to be born in wedlock. Even the most romantic lovers are finally forced by biological necessity and social pressures to agree to marry in a humdrum way, like everybody else; this was the lesson that Lydia Languish had to learn in Sheridan's *Rivals*, 400 years after Chaucer's Franklin had demonstrated much the same thing. Courtly Love was never a practicable way of life, even in courtly circles, though courtly ladies and gentlemen might pretend they were living under its fictitious dictates. This is the lesson that Chaucer teaches us in the next poem discussed.

THE 'PARLEMENT OF FOULES'

The *Parlement of Foules* is one of the most assured and satisfying of Chaucer's shorter works, and one that has been the subject of various misinterpretations. It is an occasional poem written to celebrate St. Valentine's Day, when, according to tradition, the birds meet to choose their mates for the coming year. There are innumerable examples, from later centuries, of compositions to mark festivals in much the same way; Purcell's series of *Odes to St. Cecilia* in the late 17th century is only one. Yet some critics have not thought St. Valentine excuse enough, and have tried to find occasion in the love life of the Royal Family. But since no two commentators can agree upon who the birds represent, their disagreements hardly inspire confidence in the correctness of their theories. If so many people can be made to fit, is it not more likely that no personal allusions were intended? Secondly, to seek allusions in the descriptions of the birds is to neglect the first half of the poem, which surely must be included in any account of the whole. Admittedly the last quarter, where the common birds join in the debate with their vulgar common sense, is the part that is most immediately attractive to modern ears. If we have to neglect the first three-quarters on that account, surely it is our ears that are at fault, not the poem.

The poet has been reading the *Dream of Scipio* which leads him to dream that Scipio himself came and took him to a beautiful garden where he saw the Temple of Venus, and then to a flowery hillside where all the birds had come to meet Nature on St. Valentine's Day to choose their mates. The first choice fell to a royal tercel (male) eagle, who chose the formel (female) eagle which is perched on Nature's hand; but two more tercels join in with their claims. After hearing the male eagles press their points of view, Nature throws open the case to the common birds, who have been becoming increasingly restive, but they cannot agree, so she rules that the choice must lie with the formel eagle herself, who asks for a year's grace before committing herself. After this, the common birds get on with their choosing and fly away singing in praise of the ending of winter.

The title and this account together seem to imply that the subject of the poem is the debate about which of the eagles should take the formel as his mate; but when the whole poem is taken into consideration, it appears rather to be an enquiry into the nature of love, its varieties and values, expressed by a juxtaposition of contrasted images. This may appear from an examination of the structure.

Rhetorical Construction

The poem opens with a *sententia*, a proverbial saying. This *sententia* is immediately followed by other contrasting phrases which are used to build up the idea of the duality of love. The whole is a *circumlocutio* in miniature:

> The lyf so short, the craft so long to lerne,
> Th'assay so hard, so sharp the conquerynge,
> The dredful joye, alwey that slit so yerne;   *passes quickly*
> Al this I mene by Love. . . .
>
> PARLEMENT OF FOULES 1–4

The poet has read many books about love, and one of them he read recently was 'Tully's [Cicero's] of the Dream of Scipioun'. He justifies his account by another pair of contrasting proverbs:

> For out of olde feldes, as men seyth,
> Cometh al this newe corn fro yer to yere,
> And out of olde bokes, in good feyth,
> Cometh al this newe science that men lere.   *learn*
>
> PARLEMENT OF FOULES 22–5

Scipio's dream shows a view of life that was not without great authority in the Middle Ages. It teaches the abandonment of this world in return for a heavenly reward for those who work for the common good. So it is not surprising that at the end of it the poet is disappointed, for after all he had taken up the book hoping 'a certeyn thyng to lerne'—something about love, though he does not explicitly say so. The *Dream* held out hopes of bliss for those who served the world:

But brekers of the lawe, soth to seyne,	*to say true*
And likerous folk, after that they ben dede,	*lustful*
Shul whirl aboute th'erthe alwey in peyne. . . .	

Well might he go to bed unhappy:

. . . Fulfyld of thought and busy hevynesse;	
For bothe I hadde thyng which that I nolde,	*did not want*
And ek I nadde that thyng that I wolde.	*did not have*

PARLEMENT OF FOULES 78–80, 89–91

He falls asleep and dreams that Scipio comes to him, and that is only natural since people dream at night of what they do during the day. Thus the transition is made to the main narrative by a series of proverbial sayings, just as Scipio's dream was linked to the introduction by a proverb; the account of Cicero's book is now seen to have a part to play in the structure of the poem, besides setting out the philosophy of life that is one of the poles of the contrast that is to come.

The poet and his guide come to a walled garden whose double gates bear a twofold inscription:

. . . 'Thorgh me men gon into that blysful place	
Of hertes hele and dedly woundes cure;	*healing*
Thorgh me men gon into the welle of grace,	
There grene and lusty May shal evere endure.	
This is the wey to al good aventure.	*fortune*
Be glad, thow redere, and thy sorwe of-caste;	*sorrow*
Al open am I—passe in, and sped thee faste!'	

'Thorgh me men gon', than spak that other side,
'Unto the mortal strokes of the spere
Of which Disdayn and Daunger is the gyde,

Ther nevere tre shal fruyt ne leves bere.
This strem yow ledeth to the sorweful were   *weir*
There as the fish in prysoun is al drye;
Th'eschewing is only the remedye!'   *avoidance*

PARLEMENT OF FOULES 127-40

While the modern reader probably thinks first of Virgil and
Dante before the gates of hell, not many of Chaucer's audience
would see this allusion. These inscriptions apart, it becomes clear
as the description proceeds that this is the Garden of Love, which
they would find familiar enough from the *Romance of the Rose*
and other Love Visions. The second inscription undoubtedly
refers to Courtly Love, for *Disdayn* and *Daunger* recall the personifications of the *Romance* (p. 101). *Daunger*, at any rate, is one
of the guardians of the rose, and symbolizes refusal of love,
whether from pride or obstinacy or other reason. The Wife of
Bath loved her fifth husband the most because 'he was of his love
daungerous to me'—he withheld love from her, which naturally
made her desire it the more. *Disdayn* is another word for the
same quality—in fact, in one passage of the French version of the
Romance of the Rose the two have been confused by the copyists.

The first inscription, however, celebrates natural and fruitful
love. Set against the fish trap of the second is the 'welle of grace',
and its sense of freshness and fertility is taken up by the next line:

There grene and lusty May shal evere endure.

It is in fact a 'blysful place' where all sorrows and injuries are
healed. The description of the garden bears this out; it might
almost be the Garden of Eden, or Paradise, but there is no need to
go as far as that to seek sources: the garden in the *Romance of the
Rose* was like this—perpetual balmy May, where no one grows
old or dies, and there is no night. One is irresistibly reminded of
the force of the garden image in T. S. Eliot's *Four Quartets*, where
he quotes another medieval source, St. Julian of Norwich, in his
resolution of his difficulties in a garden:

And all shall be well, and
All manner of thing shall be well.

In Chaucer's Garden of Love the minute details of description are most effective; the list of trees is brought to life by the epithets describing their use—'the saylinge fir; the cipresse, deth to playne' or again, 'the olyve of pees, and eke the dronke vyne', thus the images evoked contribute to the richness of description. The next stanza obtains its effect by the abundant use of adjectives which give enough particularity to the description to make it seem that the poet has really been there, but they are general enough, or conventional enough, to allow the reader to substitute in his own mind his favourite country places:

> A gardyn saw I ful of blosmy bowes   *branches*
> Upon a ryver, in a grene mede,
> There as swetnesse everemore inow is,   *where*   *enough*
> With floures white, blewe, yelwe, and rede,
> And colde welle-stremes, nothyng dede,
> That swymmen ful of smale fishes lighte,
> With fynnes rede and skales sylver bryghte.

PARLEMENT OF FOULES 183–9

The method of description changes as the poet moves on and comes across Cupid with his arrows; his setting is still the part of the garden we have already seen—he is 'Under a tre, besyde a welle'—but now the tone changes; the well is hardly the 'welle of grace', for it is being used to temper his arrows:

> Some for to slee, and some to wounde and kerve,   218

whereas the first inscription promised 'hertes hele and dedly woundes cure'. Cupid is accompanied by personifications who might have come straight out of the *Romance of the Rose*, and half of them are merely listed without the epithets which bring life to the previous passage. Next the poet sees the Temple of Venus, and this is made of brass, which sets it apart from the natural beauty of the garden. Inside, it proves to be a hot-house of desire fanned by jealousy, while in a remote corner lies Venus herself on a bed of gold; round the walls are portrayed the stories of unhappy lovers. The introduction of the personification is enough to show that this section is intended to portray Courtly

Love; but if more evidence is wanted, we need only point to Venus herself, who aided the dreamer in the *Romance* just as here she is shown listening to the pleas of two lovers.

The poet comes out into the fresh air again to 'the place . . . that was so sote and grene', and sees a queen whose beauty surpassed all others just as the light of the sun surpasses that of a star (and Venus, as a planet, can be called a star). This is the 'noble goddesse Nature', and she is found, not on a golden bed, but 'in a launde, upon a hill of floures':

> Of braunches were here halles and here boures
> Iwrought after here cast and here mesure. . . .
>
> PARLEMENT OF FOULES 303-4

All around her the ground is thick with birds, arranged according to rank, from the birds of prey right down to the waterfowl who sat 'lowest in the dale'. They are all listed and described by a tag, just as the trees were—we are clearly back in the mood of the opening description of the garden. Farther on, Nature is called 'the vicaire of the almighty Lord', which ties up with the 'welle of grace' of the first inscription. The birds are here by her command to choose their mates for the coming year, as they do each St. Valentine's day. This adds the final touch to the picture of natural, fruitful love according to God's commands; but no sooner do the birds begin to choose, by order of rank as is only right and proper, than we are back among the sterilities of Courtly Love, for the royal tercel eagle to whom the first choice falls replies in these words:

> . . . Unto my soverayn lady, and not my fere,   *as   mate*
> I chese, and chese with wil, and herte, and thought,
> The formel on youre hond, so wel iwrought,
> Whos I am al, and evere wol hire serve,   [*die*
> Do what hire lest, to do me lyve or sterve . . . *whatever she wishes*
>
> PARLEMENT OF FOULES 416-20

—thus making quite clear by his choice of words—'soverayn lady, and not my fere'—that he is not thinking in terms of marriage, but following the code of Courtly Love. His whole speech is full of the language of Courtly Love, and so too are the speeches of the two rival tercels who chip in with their claims. The second is of lower rank, but has served her longer; the third has not served her but is 'hire treweste man'. The position is not unlike the case in the Court of Love (p. 103), except the birds are meant to represent the common people, who can have no notion of the finer points of the code; and this they show in their comments—all except the turtle dove, with her reputation for constancy:

> 'Nay, God forbede a lovere shulde chaunge!'
> The turtle seyde, and wex for shame al red,
> 'Though that his lady everemore be straunge,   *distant*
> Yet lat hym serve hire ever, til he be ded'.

PARLEMENT OF FOULES 582–5

She thus reminds us that there is something to be said for the eagles, whereas the comments so far have varied from the common-sense, no-stuff-and-nonsense talk of the goose and duck, who say, in effect, that there are many more pebbles on the beach: the eagles whom the formel rejects should look elsewhere; to the selfish advice of the cuckoo to get a move on: as long as he gets his mate his attitude is 'I'm all right, Jack!' And none of these bits of advice has been of very much practical help. In fact, the only useful suggestion has come from the birds of prey; their spokesman said that the only way to settle the dispute was by battle, and brushing aside the suitors' eager acceptance of this, went on to say that in battle the best knight would have won, and so she ought to take the royal tercel after all! But in the end, Nature applies the closure by giving the choice to the formel herself, and she asks for a year's grace, for, as she says:

> 'I wol not serve Venus nor Cupide,
> Forsothe as yit, by no manere weye'.

PARLEMENT OF FOULES 652–3

So the common birds quickly choose their mates, and go away singing this beautiful lyric of thanksgiving at the end of the winter:

Now welcome, somer, with thy sonne softe,
That hast this wintres wedres overshake,
And driven away the longe nyghtes blake!

Saynt Valentyn, that art ful hy on-lofte,   *high above*
Thus syngen smale foules for thy sake:
Now welcome, somer, with thy sonne softe,
That hast this wintres wedres overshake.

Wel han they cause for to gladen ofte,
Sith ech of hem recovered hath hys make,   *mate*
Ful blissful mowe they synge when they wake: *may*
Now welcome, somer, with thy sonne softe,
That hast this wintres wedres overshake,
And driven away the longe nyghtes blake!

Then the poet wakes:

And with the shoutyng, whan the song was do   *was finished*
That foules maden at here flyght awey,
I wok, and othere bokes tok me to,
To reede upon, and yit I reede alwey.
I hope, ywis, to reede so som day   *indeed*
That I shal mete som thyng for to fare
The bet, and thus to reed I nyl nat spare.

PARLEMENT OF FOULES 680–99

The poem ends where it began, with the poet at his books, and
what has happened in between? The audience at the Court have
had a St. Valentine's poem with a new twist. It has dealt with a
problem of Courtly Love, as they would expect, but also with the
Dream of Scipio, with its emphasis on good works for the common profit, and with the natural love of creature for creature,
which, it is said, makes the world go round. Courtly Love has
been shown up for what it is—an amusing fantasy for the rich
and noble, but of no use whatever as a philosophy for the work-
aday world.

7

Chaucer's Works: 'Troilus and Criseyde'

Like the *Parlement of Foules*, the subject of *Troilus and Criseyde* is
love, but whereas the *Parlement* is a lighthearted gem of a piece,
the *Troilus* has been variously described as a 'tragedy'—by
Chaucer himself—or a 'psychological novel'—by some modern
critics. Both are true, for it is the most powerful of Chaucer's
works and on some counts the best. Certainly there is enough in
it to keep the commentators busy, and only a rash man would
claim to have exhausted all its meanings. I have called it the best
of his works (although some may claim that honour for some of
the *Canterbury Tales*) firstly because it is not only completed, but
also complete in itself, whereas if a tale may be thought to outshine it, it is only one gem in a necklace which has some links
broken and some stones missing. The second reason lies in the
telling of the story, and that I turn to next.

The story of *Troilus* can be set down in very few words: it is
two parts of the formula for a popular romance: 'Boy meets
girl; boy loses girl'. A more dignified, though still brief, sum-
mary comes from Speght's edition of 1598:

> In this excellent Booke is shewed the feruent loue of Troylus to
> Creseid, whome hee enjoyed for a time: and her great vntruth to
> him againe in giuing her selfe to Diomedes, who in the end did so
> cast her off that she came to great miserie. In which discourse
> Chaucer liberally treateth of the diuine purueyaunce.

This adds more; in fact, a little too much, for the story of how
Criseyde was herself deserted, which, in a way, seems a more
satisfactory ending, is now attributed to the Scot Henryson, and
not to Chaucer. It is, however, a reminder of the importance of

divine providence, which is important for the interpretation of the closing lines, which some critics have thought to be sadly out of place.

There are three main characters: Troilus, a son of Priam, King of Troy; Criseyde, the daughter of Calchas, a Trojan priest who defected to the Greeks; and Pandarus, Criseyde's uncle and Troilus' friend and companion who acts as go-between. The story takes place in Troy, during the Trojan War. It tells with exquisite irony how Troilus, who up till then had looked down on love, is suddenly struck with love for Criseyde. He pines, and Pandarus, having wormed his secret out of him, sets about bringing the two together. He overcomes Criseyde's scruples, and she, for her part, gradually comes to love Troilus in return. They enjoy perfect happiness for three years, until the Greeks (with whom her father now lives) ask for her in an exchange of prisoners of war. The code of Courtly Love forces them to keep quiet and submit to the exchange without running away together. Criseyde promises to return but finds it impossible; her timidity which made her slow to accept Troilus' advances now hinders her attempts to escape from the Greeks, until she finally succumbs to Diomedes' advances. Troilus has been distracted with grief until he learns for sure that she is unfaithful, but he is killed in battle before he can take his vengeance on Diomedes. The work finally meditates on how petty the affairs of this world are in relation to eternity.

That is the action; why does Chaucer call it a tragedy? We don't end up with a stage cluttered up with corpses as in an Elizabethan tragedy. Even the ending provided by Henryson's sequel would be more tragic. The clue comes from the prologues to the first four Books which act as milestones showing how the story is progressing. The opening lines tell us that:

> The double sorwe of Troilus to tellen,
> That was the kyng Priamus sone of Troye,
> In lovynge, how his aventures fellen   *fortune*
> Fro wo to wele, and after out of joie,   *sorrow   happiness*
> My purpos is, er that I parte fro ye.

TROILUS & CRISEYDE I, 1–5

The poem has a circular pattern; it begins with Troilus' sorrow, tells how he won his happiness, and then lost it again. His feelings, if they were plotted on a graph, would form a perfect parabola, rising to their highest point at the first consummation of their love in the middle of the third Book, almost exactly at the mid-point of the poem. All this falls well within Chaucer's own definition of tragedy, to be found in his translation of Boethius: 'Tragedye is to seyn, a dite of prosperite for a tyme that endeth in wretchydnisse'. We have been trained by later developments to expect more than this. In *King Lear* all the time of good fortune is over long before the action starts; Gloucester sums up the feeling of doom which underlies the play:

> As flies to wanton boys are we to the gods;
> They kill us for their sport.
>
> KING LEAR IV, 1, 36–7

A similar sense of the working of external forces beyond our control can be found in the *Troilus*. It shows itself in three ways, in the constant references to Fortune, in the introduction of astrological forces, and in Troilus' soliloquy on predestination in Book IV, in which he follows Boethius in all but his more favourable conclusion to prove that:

> For al that comth, comth by necessitee:
> Thus to ben lorn, it is my destinee.   *forsaken*
>
> TROILUS & CRISEYDE IV, 958–9

The image of Fortune and her revolving wheel, that both exalts the wretched and casts down the fortunate, is one of the commonplaces of the Middle Ages. Throughout the *Troilus* this image occurs again and again, particularly in the fourth book, where things are beginning to go wrong. The mood is set by the opening lines:

> But al to litel, weylaway the whyle,
> Lasteth swich joie, ythonked be Fortune,   *thanks to*
> That semeth trewest whan she wol bygyle,   *deceive*
> And kan to fooles so hire song entune,
> That she hem hent and blent, traitour comune!   *catches   blinds*

116

And whan a wight is from hire whiel ythrowe,
Than laugheth she, and maketh hym the mowe.

TROILUS & CRISEYDE IV, 1–7

This is only to be expected; but Fortune intrudes almost from the beginning. Troilus, once he has felt the pains of love, blames them on Fortune; and Pandarus retorts by saying that if her wheel stopped turning she would no longer be Fortune; so that maybe:

... she be naught fer fro thyn helpynge. *far*

I, 853

And we are left to reflect that her wheel will turn again and bring him low. Earlier still, at the moment when Troilus was struck by love, the narrator briefly outlined the whole story, using the image not of the wheel but of a flight of steps which Troilus has started to climb, little thinking that he will have to come down them again—he thought he was above love, but, you lovers, take heed from this example of what happens to those who scorn love, for:

... Love is he that alle thing may bynde,
For may no man fordon the lawe of kynde. *disobey   nature*

TROILUS & CRISEYDE I, 237–8

Thus right from the start we feel that the lovers are not entirely their own masters; at two further periods, Fortune is reinforced by the stars, as we are told at the point in Book II where the narrator explains how Criseyde came gradually to fall in love with Troilus:

And also blisful Venus, wel arrayed,
Sat in hire seventhe hous of hevene tho,
Disposed wel, and with aspectes payed,
To helpe sely Troilus of his woo.
And, sooth to seyne, she nas nat al a foo
To Troilus in his nativitee. . . .

TROILUS & CRISEYDE II, 680–5

The seventh house is not one of the signs of the Zodiac but one of the twelve fixed divisions or mansions, against which the motion of the stars can be measured: the seventh house is called the house of marriage (see p. 46). In view of this Criseyde really had no chance. Furthermore, when the critical moment comes, and Criseyde is persuaded to stay the night in Pandarus' house, she does so because of the torrential rainstorm, which is attributed to a very unusual conjunction of planets, the Moon, Saturn and Jupiter in Cancer, the sign in which the Moon has most influence.

The *Troilus* has also been called a psychological novel; so let us have a look at the way the characters are treated. The *Romance of the Rose*, as we have seen, deals with psychological states by representing them as allegorical figures. The first portion of the *Troilus* tells the same kind of story, but here we see Criseyde in person struggling with her emotions, rather than seeing her through personifications of them. All the same, Troilus starts with Belacoil; Pandarus persuades Criseyde at least to be civil to him; but there are still Daunger and the rest to be overcome. Pandarus explains her behaviour in this way:

> Peraunter thynkestow; though it be so,
> That Kynde wolde don hire to bygynne
> To have a manere routhe upon my woo,   *some pity*
> Seyth Daunger, 'Nay, thou shalt me nevere wynne!'
>
> TROILUS & CRISEYDE II, 1373-6

And just before this we have learned that she:

> . . . gan hire herte unfettre
> Out of desdaynes prison but a lite. . . .
>
> II, 1216-17

Thus the old figures of Kynde (Nature), Daunger and Disdayne are still at work in the old allegorical way, even if now they are pushed more into the background. In fact, Troilus and Criseyde are good examples of courtly lovers, and nowhere is this more clearly seen than when they refuse to run away or try to prevent their separation, because to do so would reveal their love, and this their honour forbids. Pandarus, too, fits into the pattern of the *Romance*, at least in his relations with Troilus, whose friend, confidant, and mentor he is. In this he is acting the part of the

118

allegorical figure, Frend, from the *Romance*. Frend helps and advises the dreamer, and this is what Pandarus does for Troilus, all the while laying stress on their friendship.

From this account it might be thought that the three characters are no more than lifeless puppets acting out the old stories, but the magic of it is in the way they are brought alive. We feel that we are reading about real people, and though what they do may be a little strange at times, yet they 'spedde as wel in love as men do now'. This comes about partly from the mention of small quirks of character, and partly from the humorous way in which the story is told. We can see it in the way Pandarus is made to be unsuccessful in his own loves, and in the colloquial teasing words of Troilus:

'This were a wonder thing,' quod Troilus.	*remarkable*
'Thow koudest nevere in love thiselven wisse:	*succeed*
How devel maistow brynge me to blisse?'	

I, 621–3

We see another touch of humanity in the way Criseyde does not like to ask if the rumours of her exchange are true:

| But shortly, lest thise tales sothe were, | *true* |
| She dorst at no wight asken it, for fere. | |

IV, 671–2

which bears out the earlier description of her as the 'ferfulleste wight' in Book II.

These are only a few examples; the biggest proof of how the lovers come alive is the shock that comes in the middle of Book V when they are described fully for the first time, because they have seemed to us so real without our being told what they look like. It is because they have become so real to us that they seem like old friends; it is because of this that we feel for them and identify ourselves with them in joy and sorrow; this is why the recitation of their distress can move us to the verge of tears. In view of this involvement the ending comes as something of a relief, when we are reminded that for those who believe in Christ and his redemption of the world there can be no such thing as a tragedy, for the affairs of this world count for nothing in comparison with the prospects of eternity. The ending is not just a pious afterthought, as often stated, but rather the equivalent of Milton's sense of 'calm of mind, all passion spent' which gives such a satisfying conclusion to *Samson Agonistes*. Here are two of the last stanzas:

> O yonge, fresshe folkes, he or she,
> In which that love up groweth with youre age,
> Repeyreth hom fro worldly vanyte,   *turn*
> And of youre herte up casteth the visage
> To thilke God that after his ymage
> Yow made, and thynketh al nys but a faire
> This world, that passeth soone as floures faire.
>
> And loveth hym, the which that right for love
> Upon a crois, oure soules for to beye,   *redeem*
> First starf, and roos, and sit in hevene above;   *died*
> For he nyl falsen no wight, dar I seye,
> That wol his herte al holly on hym leye.
> And syn he best to love is, and most meke,
> What nedeth feynede loves for to seke?

TROILUS & CRISEYDE V, 1835–48

To modern ears this seems like a conventional gesture to the Church, or to Christianity: but to think this is not to understand either Chaucer or the age in which he lived, an age in which the builders of our great cathedrals could without a feeling of incongruity incorporate pagan and secular fables and figures into the stonework, and yet build entirely to the glory of God. This consideration should prevent us also from thinking that Chaucer was not perfectly sympathetic to his lovers as he tells their moving story.

8

Chaucer's Works: The 'Canterbury Tales'

The *Canterbury Tales* is the one work which anyone who has read any Chaucer at all is bound to have sampled. It is the work upon which his modern reputation depends, and yet I have only mentioned it in passing so far. This is deliberate; the discussion of his earlier works was intended to show that the *Canterbury Tales* was not written in a vacuum, to emerge suddenly as the first monument of English poetry, and also to show that there are other poems by Chaucer besides the *Tales* which merit our attention today. But before going on to examine the *Tales* in detail in the rest of this chapter, at the risk of seeming repetitious I am going to return briefly to the earlier works to pick out explicitly a theme which runs through them, and which has so far been implied rather than stated clearly.

The point which I want to bring out is the growing importance of the juxtaposition of contrasting elements in Chaucer's writings as his style matured. There is a possible analogy here with contemporary art, or at least architecture. The predominant architectural style during Chaucer's lifetime was what is now known as the *Gothic*. It had its origins in France in the 12th century and lasted until the Renaissance. In architecture, both the Romanesque style which preceded it and the classical revival which came later were founded upon the harmony produced by the use of the classical orders of architecture. Every building seemed to have a rational scheme imposed upon it. Gothic architecture, on the other hand, is covered all over with unrestrained decoration: detail is piled upon detail. Instead of the squatter, more solid-seeming barrel vault, the vaults of a Gothic church seem to soar upwards airily towards the heavens: there is a flood of light because the window area has been greatly increased. This was all made possible by the calculation and balancing of opposing stresses. The sculpture with which the buildings were decorated shared this tendency; poses became more fluid: an outstretched foot was balanced by a turn of the head. Expression also became far more naturalistic. The same is true in painting, which now became far more decorative, and displayed a wealth of realistic detail. Moreover, several aspects or stages of an event were shown in the same picture. (See the miniature illustrated after p. 72, showing Charles d'Orleans both imprisoned in the Tower, and also leaving London in the background.) One art-historian (Arnold Hauser, quoted by Muscatine in *Chaucer and the French Tradition*, pp. 167–8) has said:

> The basic form of Gothic art is juxtaposition. . . . The beholder is, as it were, led through the stages and stations of a journey. . . . In painting it is the 'continuous' method which is favoured; the drama strives to make the episodes as complete as possible, and prefers, instead of the concentration of the action in a few decisive situations, frequent changes of scene, of the characters and the motifs. . . .

The old way of looking at Chaucer's literary development was to see it divided into three distinct periods: French, Italian and English. That is to say that he started off by imitating French poets; that he went to Italy on business and was struck with Italian poetry, so that he started using Italian models instead of French, and that finally he threw off foreign influences and in his English period became truly himself. This is a gross simplification, and one that relies perhaps on a belief in the sort of sudden conversion St. Paul experienced on the road to Damascus, and on the theory that what is new is necessarily superior.

GOTHIC CONTRAST IN CHAUCER

A more fruitful way of looking at his career is to see it as an increasing Gothic mastery of contrast and juxtaposition, which are the foundations of the ironic humour for which he is justly celebrated. We must start again from the *Romance of the Rose*;

this was his own starting-point, and its style formed one of the poles of the contrasts in his later work. The first portion of the French original—the part he translated—is in the style of a romance of Courtly Love, and in form it is in the love-vision tradition, which according to Robinson is marked by:

> ... the discussion of sleeplessness and dreams, the setting on May-day or in the spring-time, the vision itself, the guide (who in many poems takes the form of a helpful animal), the personified abstractions, Love, Fortune, Nature, and the like.

266

Another way of looking at the love-vision is to see it as an organic structure in which certain actions take place before the main part of the story is reached. The time is spring; after some difficulty the narrator falls asleep, and dreams that he is in a beautiful landscape, which he describes; next he encounters a series of figures, either painted or real, which he describes, after which he meets his guide. It is at this point that the story proper is ready to begin.

The *Book of the Duchess*, developing from the *Romance of the Rose*, shows the first glimmerings of that naturalistic style which is said to be the hall-mark of Chaucer's later poetry. Most of the poem is written in the same conventional courtly vein as his translation of the *Romance*, but there are touches of comic naturalism as well as observed detail which are not to be found in that work. Apart from the portrayal of the narrator himself, one notable passage is the one where Iris is sent on a message to Morpheus, the God of Sleep:

> This messager com fleynge faste
> And cried, 'O, ho! awake anoon!'
> Hit was for noght; there herde hym non.
> 'Awake!' quod he, 'who ys lyth there?'
> And blew his horn ryght in here eere,
> And cried 'Awaketh!' wonder hyë.   *very loud*
> This god of slep with hys oon yë
> Cast up, axed, 'Who clepeth ther?'   *calls*

123

'Hyt am I,' quod this messager.   '*It's me!*'
'Juno bad thow shuldest goon'. . . .

BOOK OF THE DUCHESS 178–87

Here barrack-room realism is suddenly inserted in a romantic dream, and the humour inherent in the notion that the God of Sleep should be very hard to waken is increased by the contrast. In a second passage, detailed observation gives us the impression that we are listening to a description of something that really happened. When we read that the narrator comes across a puppy and

> Hyt com and crepte to me as lowe
> Ryght as hyt hadde me yknowe,
> Helde doun hys hed and joyned hys eres,
> And leyde al smothe doun hys heres.

BOOK OF THE DUCHESS 391–4

we can recognize, in that detail, typical canine behaviour, and this again lends an air of reality to the whole.

The *Parlement of Foules* shows both these sorts of realism in better balance with the rest. We have already noted the realism produced by the minuteness of the descriptions of the garden, and by the outbursts of the common birds against the courtly ones. In the debate in particular the contrasted styles play each other off and enhance the effect of each; this passage gives us one of the juxtapositions of images which, as we saw, makes up the poem. To the rudimentary contrasts of mere style in the *Duchess*, the *Parlement* adds contrasts of images and subject-matter.

Troilus and Criseyde is not a love-vision like the previous poems, but in it the technique of contrast reaches a new level. Courtly Love represented by Troilus is set against Pandarus' practical materialism, and both against the Divine Love of the closing stanzas. Here Chaucer seems in complete control of his material: the courtly and the colloquial are in harmony, and the balance he hit in the second half of the *Parlement* is maintained throughout.

Finally we come to the *Canterbury Tales*, the story, as everyone knows, of a pilgrimage to Canterbury. It falls into two parts: in the *Prologue*, the scene is set, the pilgrims described, and the foundations laid for the rest of the story, which consists of the tales themselves and the linking passages between them. It is the one work upon which Chaucer's popular reputation depends, the foundation stone and first monument of English literature. Yet it is superior to the *Troilus* not so much in quality of inspiration, as in width of range; the naturalistic elements have far wider scope than in the more serious poem.

THE 'PROLOGUE' AS A LOVE-VISION

At first sight its connections with Chaucer's earlier work may not be at all apparent, but, in fact, it is possible to see the *Prologue* as an adaptation of the love-vision. This is obscured because in the interests of realism, and of seeming to be describing an actual pilgrimage as it took place, Chaucer cannot afford any suspicion of unreality that a dream would introduce. What seems to have happened is that he took up the traditional sequence of events at the point at which the dreamer begins to tell his dream. At least, the narrator begins by describing the lushness of the countryside in spring (mid-April, to be precise), goes on to describe a group of figures (albeit living ones), meets his guide (the Host), and then the main story begins. One might object that this is such a refined version of the love-vision opening that all substance has been refined away. A comparison with the opening lines of the *Romance* may, however, yield quite unsuspected results: (For the opening of the *Prologue*, see p. 9.)

> . . . That it was May, thus dremed me,
> In tyme of love and jolite,
> That al thing gynneth waxen gay,   *begins to grow gay*
> For ther is neither busk nor hay   *bush   hedge*
> In May, that it nyl shrouded ben,   *will not*
> And it with newe leves wren.   *clothed*
> These wodes eek recoveren grene,
> That drie in wynter ben to sene;
> And the erthe wexith proud withalle,
> For swote dewes that on it falle, . . .   *sweet*
> . . . Hard is the hert that loveth nought

In May, whan al this mirth is wrought,
Whan he may on these braunches here
The smale briddes syngen clere   *birds*
Her blisful swete song pitous.

ROMANCE OF THE ROSE 51–60, 85–9

and off the dreamer goes at the start of his adventure in search of
love. This comparison—and the full passage is even more reveal-
ing—makes it seem not unlikely that Chaucer took the old
tradition and moulded it to his own purposes. At least even the
most assiduous source hunters have not turned up any more convincing explanation of the framework of the *Tales*, and have
been reduced to supposing that the theme of a pilgrimage occurred to Chaucer because he lived for a time in Greenwich on
the Canterbury road and thus must have been familiar with the
sight of pilgrims passing his house. This is really putting the cart
before the horse. It is probably truer to say that an artist can only
see what his artistic tradition tells him is there. How many
people have ever noticed that the shadows on snow are blue
before seeing that this is how an artist paints them?

The *Canterbury Tales* contains within itself all the contrasts
noted in its predecessors, though its greater size permits their
application on a larger scale. The *Book of the Duchess* had short
episodes of realism like the Morpheus one (p. 123); the *Tales* has
the *Miller's Tale* set against the courtly bulk of the *Knight's Tale*.
This is one example of the form that the contrast between the
courtly and the colloquial may take; others we will come to
later. Then there are the contrasts in love, not only in the so-
called 'Marriage Group' (see p. 136), but also within a single
character—what sort of love, for instance, does the Prioress mean
by her *Amor vincit omnia* badge? And with this question of love
is bound up the image of the pilgrimage itself. A full treatment
of this theme must await the more fundamental question of
Chaucer's powers of description and their part in the illusion of
realism.

CHAUCER'S DESCRIPTIVE METHOD

The correct way of describing an object or person was laid down in manuals of rhetoric (pp. 79–83). A description was an easy way of padding out inadequate material, and there was no shortage of prescribed methods and of stock descriptions. In general, a subject's moral nature was separated from his physical characteristics, which were described in a specified order working from head to toe, followed by an account of his clothing. A good example of the stock method is the description of Lycurgus in the *Knight's Tale* (2130–54). He is an invented symbolical figure; not so Blanche, the wife of John of Gaunt, who is described in the *Book of the Duchess*. A part of her description runs like this:

> And goode faire White she het;
> That was my lady name ryght.
> She was bothe fair and bryght;
> She hadde not hir name wrong.
> Ryght faire shuldres and body long
> She had, and armes, every lyth   *limb*
> Fattyssh, flesshy, not gret therwith
> Ryght white handes, and nayles rede,
> Round brestes; and of good brede   *width*
> Hyr hippes were, a streight flat back.

BOOK OF THE DUCHESS 948–57

Admittedly it is an idealized portrait, and I have only quoted a small part, yet there is hardly a single personal touch in the whole. The same is true, as might be expected, of the descriptions of the allegorical figures in the opening of the *Romance of the Rose*. This was Chaucer's point of departure. The figures are all that might be expected from a consideration of what they stand for. They are complete down to Avarice's last rag and well-filled purse. Let us now turn to the end of Chaucer's career so that the differences attributable to his development may stand out the more clearly.

Many of the figures in the *General Prologue* seem almost to leap out of the page. There are two reasons for this. The first is that the descriptions follow no set order; items appear to tumble out just as they come into the narrator's mind. The effect is as if we were listening to an eye-witness pouring out his news without pausing to reflect and to rearrange it in a logical order. Take the

Wife of Bath; from what we hear about her, she appears to be an extroverted, hearty sort of person, not unlike a Bradford woolman of today. On top of this she is deaf, which probably only makes her and everyone else shout louder. It must have been one of the most noticeable things about her, and so it is blurted out at once:

> A good wif was ther of biside Bathe,
> But she was somdel deef, and that was scathe.   *rather   a pity*
> Of clooth-makyng she hadde swich an haunt,   *skill*
> She passed hem of Ypres and of Gaunt.
> In al the parisshe wif ne was ther noon
> That to the offrynge bifore hire sholde goon;
> And if ther dide, certeyn so wrooth was she,
> That she was out of alle charitee.

CT: GEN. PROL. I, 445–52

Only after her deafness comes her skill at weaving, about which she would not have been slow to tell the company on every possible occasion, and after that her self-importance. This passage also illustrates the second reason for the liveliness of Chaucer's descriptions: his way of converting the portrait of a type into one of an individual typical of a class by adding distinctive personal details—the Wife of Bath's deafness, and later, her fine scarlet stockings. Even brief portraits can include significant detail: the Yeoman has his St. Christopher medallion, and the Cook has his ulcer, just as the Prioress, who is described at length, has her pet dogs. The most individual treatment is not reserved for those who merit the longest portraits, but rather for those who are at the lower end of the moral scale, or those whose person does not seem to be entirely in harmony with their office. The Parson, on the other hand, is described at length; he is set up as an exemplar, but about his personal characteristics as a real man we learn comparatively little.

THE SIGNIFICANCE OF THE PILGRIMAGE

The people who are described in the *General Prologue* are about to set out on a pilgrimage, and this fact is perhaps more significant than would appear at first glance. Its obvious practical significance is that it provides Chaucer with a piece of machinery for getting this queer assortment of people together. The thirty or so pilgrims are, in fact, a fair sample of society in general, with the exception of the upper end—the nobility who would make their pilgrimages with their households instead of joining as it were a package tour—and those at the bottom who could not afford to go. Here are representatives of Church and laity; countrymen and townsmen; the professions, commerce and the military. The pilgrimage is the motive that unites them, providing a natural explanation of why and how they should be travelling together, which forestalls any awkward questions from the audience; a pilgrimage was the only occasion when such a varied crowd would share a common purpose and be forced into intimacy with each other.

But perhaps more significantly, on a symbolic level the image of a pilgrimage ties up with the question of love, which has been one of the constant themes of Chaucer's works. A pilgrimage should remind us of the Divine Love; the figure of life as a pilgrimage towards the Divine Love is as old as the Church herself. St. Paul writes of us as strangers and pilgrims in this world; Dante's *Divine Comedy* tells of another sort of pilgrimage, as it were 'Nel mezzo del cammin di nostra vita' (along the road of our life); and Chaucer's Parson himself links the pilgrimage to Canterbury with the pilgrimage of life:

> And Jhesu, for his grace, wit me sende
> To shewe yow the wey, in this viage,
> Of thilke parfit glorious pilgrymage
> That highte Jerusalem celestial.

CT: PARSON'S PROL. X, 48–51

This is the religious aspect of the pilgrimage, the journey undertaken in obedience to Divine Love. But it is springtime; new life and vigour are returning to nature. Besides the pull of the saints there is the clamour of the birds;

> . . . And smale foweles maken melodye,
> That slepen al the nyght with open ye. . . .

This is the insistent sound that awakens thoughts of secular love in men's hearts. Remember the *Romance of the Rose*:

> Hard is the hert that loveth nought
> In May, whan al this mirth is wrought. . . .

When we look more closely at the motives of each of the pilgrims, we can see both kinds of love at work. The Knight, it is safe to assume, responded to the religious call: '. . . he loved chivalrie,/Trouthe and honour, fredom and curteisie', and had come straight from the wars, all travel-stained as he was, to 'doon his pilgrymage'. But what about the Squire? His portrait is idealized too, but

> So hoote he lovede that by nyghtertale
> He sleep namoore than dooth a nyghtyngale.

CT: GEN. PROL. I, 97-8

He had no more inclination to sleep than had the birds; is there any doubt that, with his 'hope to stonden in his lady grace', his intentions were anything but secular? The Wife of Bath is another for whom the religious exercises are not the main purpose of her journey. This is only hinted at in the *Prologue* where we are led to believe that her aim in her church-going is only to display herself, but in the prologue to her tale her philosophy of life is stated unequivocally. Whereas the Squire is governed by the ideal of Courtly Love, she looks not to God but to Venus. She is at heart a pagan, and travelling to find herself yet another husband.

The motives of some of the other pilgrims seem rather ambiguous. Take the Prioress. Whereas the Parson is described not by personal detail but by the way in which he carries out his office, she is described as a woman—and in courtly terms at that—and we are left to wonder about her performance as prioress. Her name is Eglantyne, a name for the heroine of a romance; but she is a nun. 'Symple and coy' have strong overtones of Courtly Love; but they can legitimately be used in a religious context. She sings attractively; but it is the divine service she sings to the greater glory of God. She is tender-hearted; but her compassion seems to be directed more towards animals than her fellow men. Her wimple is smartly pleated; but it is the regulation dress. She carries a string of coral beads; but they are a rosary. Her badge reads 'Love conquers all'; but this may be said of both secular and divine love. Again, contrast is the key.

The scene is now set and the guide appears. The Host himself joins the party as a cross between a courier and master of ceremonies. As the journey gets under way, the characters who have been described in a series of static poses now begin to interact on one another, and the illusion of reality is helped by the actions of the pilgrims themselves. They have become, as it were, actors in a drama. This is put in motion as they pause to draw lots for who is to tell the first tale. As is fitting, the lot falls to the Knight: he ought to take precedence over all the others. And with this the *Prologue* ends.

THE 'KNIGHT'S TALE'

We have already looked at the *Knight's Tale* from one perspective in Chapter 3 (pp. 52–7). There it was the astrological theory behind the poem that was of interest, and not the telling of the tale or its position in the larger scheme of the whole work. Many modern critics have found difficulty in this and have tried to place the meaning of the tale in the plot or in the characterization. There is not a great deal of story, and what there is hardly moves at a brisk pace throughout; and as for the characterization, the two heroes are as alike as two peas in a pod. If one takes them as an allegory of the active versus the contemplative life, it is a toss-up which represents which, nor is it any easier to draw a moral from the conclusion. The difficulty arises when we try to approach the tale from the naturalistic standpoint, which is appropriate enough for the *General Prologue* which immediately precedes it. From the *Prologue* we gain a strong impression of modernity; but if we expect the first tale to do so as well, and apply the same criteria to it, we are bound to be disappointed. A likelier explanation seems to lie in the person of the Knight himself; to this extent the tale is determined by the demands of realism. He is a knight, long schooled in courtly manners; as a

Squire he must have spent afternoons and evenings entertaining the company 'in talking of chronicles of kinges, and of other actes marcealls'. The style which comes naturally to him is not the colloquialism of a bawdy folk-tale, but the slow courtly style of the French romances, which we have already traced through Chaucer's poetry. We ought to expect, then, a slow-moving richly coloured pageant to while away the empty hours as pleasantly as possible. The pace is slow, deliberately slow, far too slow for modern tastes attuned to short action-packed novels; it would have been more in keeping with the taste of a century ago in the days of more leisurely writing and the three-decker novel. Not only are there lengthy and lavish descriptions of scenery and people—take those of Lycurgus and Emetrius, who play a minute part in the actual action—not only are speeches long and in part redundant by naturalistic standards—Venus surely knows by this time what Saturn's powers are—but also when time is mentioned it is often the passage of a long period that is stressed.

The second point to notice about the tale is its symmetry. The earthly actors are matched by the heavenly forces; there is very little to choose between Palamon and Arcite; even the lists are round and symmetrically constructed; the temples balance each other, and so do the prayers made in each of them; Palamon and Arcite first fight in the same spot that is to be the site of the tournament in the lists and of Arcite's funeral rites. All in all, the tale is an exercise in courtly romance, and this is how the audience takes it:

> Whan that the Knyght had thus his tale ytoold,
> In al the route nas ther yong ne oold
> That he ne seyde it was a noble storie,
> And worthy for to drawen to memorie;
> And namely the gentils everichon.   *especially*
>
> CT: MILLER'S PROL. I, 3109–13

THE 'MILLER'S' AND THE 'REEVE'S' TALES

After that stately tale comes yet another contrast. We move from ancient Athens to modern Oxford; the next tale is the Miller's, a rollicking one about how an aged carpenter with a young and beautiful wife was duped and cuckolded by his lodger, who in the end went too far. The courtly is followed by the naturalistic. But the thing to observe is the skill by which Chaucer engineers the contrast. The Host invites the Monk to tell the next tale, but before he can begin, the Miller butts his way in, blind drunk, and the Host, whose experience of drunks must be considerable, has to let him have his own way:

> The Millere, that for dronken was al pale. . .
> . . . in Pilates voys he gan to crie,
> And swoor, 'By armes, and by blood and bones,
> I kan a noble tale for the nones,
> With which I wol now quite the Knyghtes tale.'   *repay*
> Oure Hooste saugh that he was dronke of ale,
> And seyde, 'Abyd, Robyn, my leeve brother;   *Hold on dear*
> Som bettre man shal telle us first another.
> Abyd, and lat us werken thriftily.'
>   'By Goddes soule,' quod he, 'that wol nat I;
> For I wol speke, or elles go my wey.'
> Oure Hoost answerde, 'Tel on, a devel wey!
> Thou art a fool; thy wit is overcome.'
> CT: MILLER'S PROL. I, 3120, 3124–35

The Miller now states his subject, and this only rouses the Reeve who is himself a carpenter by trade like the duped husband. Thus when the Miller comes to the end of his tale, the Reeve has to get his own back, and tell of how a miller was worsted. But even though his tale is told for revenge, it is not introduced in the rumbustious way suited to the Miller, who breaks down doors with his head. The Reeve is old and nurses grievances within himself until the time to strike—his fellow villagers were 'adrad of him as of the deeth'. So after a touching soliloquy on the troubles of old age, he begins, his malice controlled, but none the less there. It only breaks out in the last line of the tale, consorting rather oddly with his final prayer:

> And God, that sitteth heighe in magestee,
> Save al this compaignye, grete and smale!
> Thus have I quyt the Millere in my tale.   *paid out*
> CT: REEVE'S TALE I, 4322–4

This sequence is continued by the Cook, who chips in with his praise of the Reeve's tale, and after a little badinage with the Host starts a tale about an innkeeper. However, it hardly has begun before the manuscript breaks off, and this first section of the *Canterbury Tales* (as we have them) comes to an end.

THE 'REALITY' OF THE PILGRIMS

From the foregoing it can be seen how Chaucer employs contrast, and how, in doing so, he brings his characters to life by showing them interacting on each other. The result is that we feel that they are real people; and this feeling is reinforced by a device he uses twice (once at the end of the *General Prologue*, and once before the *Miller's Tale*): to disclaim any responsibility for what he is about to relate:

> For this ye knowen al so wel as I,
> Whoso shal telle a tale after a man
> He moot reherce as ny as evere he kan,   *repeat*
> Everich a word, if it be in his charge,
> Al speke he never so rudeliche and large,
> Or ellis he moot telle his tale untrewe,
> Or feyne thyng, or fynde wordes newe.   *falsify*
>
> CT: GEN. PROL. I, 730–6

Such a disclaimer makes it appear doubly certain that the pilgrimage actually took place, and is not merely a product of Chaucer's imagination.

This seeming reality of the pilgrims has encouraged a search for actual people who could have served as prototypes. There was a spate of activity in this field in the first quarter of this century, and several very plausible identifications have been made, particularly by J. M. Manly in his book *Some New Light on Chaucer* which was published in 1926. He points out, for example, a Thomas Pynchbek as a model for the Man of Law; Sir John Bussy as the Franklin; John Hawley as the Shipman. These and the other identifications he gives are admirable examples of persistent and skilled detective work. But they hardly advance our critical understanding or appreciation of the poem.

The information that has been so laboriously dug up is irrelevant. It is one matter to discover the functions of the pilgrims; their place in society has a bearing on the way they might be expected to behave, and knowing this, we can then see how Chaucer has shown them behaving, and appreciate the better what he is trying to do. But the discovery that certain of the pilgrims were drawn from life is not so helpful. Granted that for Chaucer's immediate audience the introduction of a well-known figure thinly disguised as a pilgrim would undoubtedly have added a piquancy to their reception of the poem, nevertheless it is not an effect that can be reproduced at will today from the knowledge that such a person certainly existed and his career followed a certain course. Nothing short of personal acquaintance is really sufficient. For us the characters will have to stand or fall on their own merits as pieces of characterization.

Another reason to distrust these identifications is that they have been made on the assumption that Chaucer would more or less mechanically reproduce his models without altering them, so that they remain recognizable six centuries later. This certainly would make any search easier, but it discounts Chaucer's artistry. We can demonstrate this on the one pilgrim who was undoubtedly known personally to Chaucer's audience. This is, of course, Chaucer himself, and we can do this because, through his writings, we can see what sort of person he was, and compare this with the picture he gives of himself. Now he does not show himself in a very favourable light; he appears to be somewhat naïve and slow on the uptake; furthermore he has no experience or success in love. For example, look at his fumbling and insensitive questioning of the Man in Black in the *Book of the Duchess*; at the poor opinion of his intellect held by the Eagle in the *House of Fame*. In the *Parlement of Foules*, he is unceremoniously bundled into the garden by Scipio on the grounds that he should have nothing to fear as the inscriptions are intended only for those that 'Loves servaunt be'. And, as he said at the beginning, 'I knowe nat love in dede'. Throughout his works he presents himself as a self-effacing, rather simple observer, and this is true of the *Canterbury Tales* as well. But his poetry is certainly not the product of a naïve or slow mind, nor would he have been sent on important foreign missions, or kept his post at the Customs if he was the sort of person he portrays himself as. Unfortunately we have no information of his performance in affairs of the heart, but it is far more likely from his obviously ironic cast of mind that in this too he would show himself proficient. In the same way, when he comes to tell his own story on the pilgrimage, he doesn't pull his best one out of reserve, but instead starts off on a piece of the worst hack work, until we have the ironic situation of a poet who has found a favourable audience at Court being stopped by a mere innkeeper:

> 'Namoore of this, for Goddes dignitee,'
> Quod oure Hooste, 'for thou makest me
> So wery of thy verray lewednesse   *ignorance*
> That, also wisly my God my soule blesse,
> Myne eres aken of thy drasty speche.   *worthless*
>
> CT: SIR THOPAS VII, 919–23 (B 2109–13)

Chaucer's self-portrait is the one place where we can see his methods at work most clearly, and his way of exploiting the humour in his material to the utmost, a humour that the labours of the detectives seem to pay too little attention to.

THE 'MARRIAGE DEBATE'

This humour Chaucer exploits by the dramatic relationships between the pilgrims. We have already looked at the first group of tales and the way in which they are related. This is only a short section of the whole, and there are only two main actors, the Miller and the Reeve. Later on in the work a more sustained relationship may be seen which links seven tales, those of the Wife of Bath, Friar, Summoner, Clerk, Merchant, Squire and Franklin. These tales constitute what is generally known as the 'Marriage Group' or 'Marriage Debate', because they exemplify different relationships between husband and wife.

The debate runs as follows: before she tells her tale, the Wife of Bath lays bare her heart and explains with some gusto her philosophy of life. She is in favour of marriage; the more the better, in fact, provided that the wife wears the trousers. She ought to know; she has had five husbands in her time, the last being a clerk from Oxford, and is now ready for her sixth (though one would think that the way she says she treated them would be enough to put any thinking man off!). Her tale continues this theme; her hero, when set to discover what it is that women desire most, returns with the answer:

> . . . 'Wommen desiren to have sovereynetee
> As wel over hir housbond as hir love,
> And for to been in maistrie hym above.
> This is youre mooste desir. . . .'

CT: WIFE OF BATH'S TALE III, 1038–41

The Clerk is understandably upset by her heresy and her clerkly way of using authorities to prove it (see the *Parson's Tale* for an example of the real thing), by her animalism and attitude to marriage, and by the treatment of her last husband, like himself a clerk of Oxford. But before he can reply, Chaucer inserts the quarrel between the Friar and Summoner as a dramatic interlude in the interests of realism, just as the Miller butted his way in earlier. Eventually the Clerk replies to the Wife of Bath by a tale he learnt from Petrarch, another clerk, about a wife who remained constant and uncomplaining through the worst adversity; he brings this home to the Wife of Bath in an ironic epilogue which exhorts wives to treat their husbands as the Wife of Bath suggests, and make them unhappy as she did. The Merchant takes up the Clerk's last line; he has been unhappily married for two months, and his tale, beginning with an ironic encomium on marriage, can be taken as an attack on the institution altogether. Another interlude, an (incomplete) tale of pure romance from the Squire, is followed by the final tale in which the Franklin reconciles the opposing points of view by telling how a couple lived in happiness, each respecting the other without seeking to dominate.

This is a bald description of the debate; longer ones are in general far more convincing, more convincing even than a reading of Chaucer's text. It is on occasions like this, where what is under consideration is the effect an author produces on his readers, that a reading of the text itself is worth a dozen critical arguments. I am in a minority here and stand to be corrected by those who have read the *Canterbury Tales* with due attention, but I find it hard to see in the text justification for the 'marriage debate' which its supporters adduce. I rest my case on a reading of the tales, but there is one preliminary consideration; the *Canterbury Tales* as we have them today, were never finished. The original plan, as set out in the *General Prologue*, calls for 120 tales, four each from thirty pilgrims; we have only two dozen, and their order and relationships are still a matter for debate. It is not at all hard to show, as I have done, how the sequence from the *General Prologue* to the *Cook's Tale* is held together. It forms a coherent group in all the manuscripts, and apart from the connection of subject between the *Miller's* and the *Reeve's Tales*, each tale is explicitly connected with those on each side by the link passages. And in general the best evidence for the relationships between the pilgrims comes from the links and interruptions where they are shown acting directly upon one another; it is the links that chiefly show the purpose a pilgrim had in telling his tale:

> This dronke Millere hath ytoold us heer
> How that bigyled was a carpenteer,
> Peradventure in scorn, for I am oon.
> And, by youre leve, I shal hym quite anoon. . . .
>
> CT: REEVE'S PROL. I, 3913–16

> O Lord, oure Lord, thy name how merveilous . . .
>
> . . . .
>
> | Wherfore in laude, as I best kan or may, | *praise* |
> |---|---|
> | Of thee and of the white lylye flour | *lily* |
> | Which that the bar, and is a mayde alway, | *who bore you* |
> | To telle a storie I wol do my labour. . . . | |
>
> CT: PRIORESS'S PROL. VII, 453–63 (B1643–53)

> This Persoun answerde, al atones,
> 'Thou getest fable noon ytoold for me. . . .
>
> . . . .
>
> | For which I seye, if that yow list to heere | *if it please you* |
> |---|---|
> | Moralitee and vertuous mateere, | |

138

And thanne that ye wol yeve me audience,
I wol ful fayn, at Christes reverence,
Do yow plesaunce leefful, as I kan.   *give you legitimate pleasure*
                              CT: PARSON'S PROL. X, 30–41

Those are three examples; in them the purpose of the tales is
conveyed far more clearly than in the tales themselves. In
fact, the evidence of the tales may even be deceptive, as not all
of them have been finally tailored to fit their tellers. The narrator
of the *Shipman's Tale* seems to be a woman, and that of the
Second Nun's a man.

Now, bearing in mind that the 'Marriage Group' is divided
among three separate portions in the manuscripts, and that the
order of these portions is not entirely certain, and that in any case
the *Canterbury Tales* were never completed, let us see how these
seven tales are linked together. The quarrel between the Friar
and Summoner connects their two tales by their themes, but this
is made explicit by the links:

> . . . I wol yow of a somonour telle a game.
>   CT: FRIAR'S PROL. III, 1279
> This Somonour in his styropes hye stood;
> Upon this Frere his herte was so wood   *enraged*
> That lyke an aspen leef he quook for ire.
>   CT: SUMMONER'S PROL. III, 1665–7

These two tales are joined to the *Wife of Bath's Tale*, which
precedes them, by the Friar's approving remarks on her preaching style; there is no link with the preceding group, nor with the
Clerk's Tale, which comes next. There is, however, a reference
back right at the end, after he has emphasized the moral of his
story:

> This storie is seyd, nat for that wyves sholde
> Folwen Grisilde as in humylitee,
> For it were inportable, though they wolde;   *impossible*
> But for that every wight, in his degree,
> Sholde be constant in adversitee
> As was Grisilde; therfore Petrak writeth
> This storie, which with heigh stile he enditeth.   *composes*

> For, sith a womman was so pacient   *since*
> Unto a mortal man, wel moore us oghte
> Receyven al in gree that God us sent. . . .
>
> CT: CLERK'S TALE IV, 1142–51

In other words, as we might expect from its teller, this tale is intended as an example of heavenly virtues, not as a shot in a worldly battle about marriage, for the theme of the tale, like that of the *Book of Job*, is patience in adversity. It is only after this that the Clerk alters his tone and brings in the Wife of Bath:

> For which heere, for the Wyves love of Bathe—
> Whos lyf and al hire secte God mayntene   *sex*
> In heigh maistrie, and elles were it scathe—   *a pity*
> I wol with lusty herte, fressh and grene,
> Seyn yow a song to glade yow, I wene;
> And lat us stynte of ernestful matere.   *leave off   serious*
> Herkneth my song that seith in this manere. . . .
>
> CT: CLERK'S TALE IV, 1170–6

There then follows his ironic song which encourages wives to act like the Wife of Bath, and ends with a reference to what their husbands will suffer:

> And lat hym care, and wepe, and wrynge, and waille!
>
> CT: CLERK'S TALE IV, 1212

This is the only link between the two halves, and it comes, not in a link passage immediately after the *Wife of Bath's Tale*, where it might have been expected, but in an explicitly light-hearted section at the end of the *Clerk's Tale*. Compare the way in which the *Merchant's Tale* is introduced. The first line of his tale picks up the last line of the Clerk's:

> 'Wepyng and waylyng, care and oother sorwe
> I knowe ynogh, on even and a-morwe',
> Quod the Marchant. . . .
>
> CT: MERCHANT'S PROL. IV, 1213–15

His wife, alas, is quite different from Griselda:

> She is a shrew at al.   *completely*
> Ther is a long and large difference
> Bitwix Grisildis grete pacience
> And of my wyf the passing crueltee.   *surpassing*
> CT: CLERK'S TALE IV, 1222-5

And yet in seventeen manuscripts the *Clerk's* and the *Merchant's Tales* are separated, which goes to show how chancy the order of the tales is. The *Squire's Tale* follows, but there is no formal link with the *Merchant's Tale*, though there is with the *Franklin's Tale*, which comes next and concludes the so-called 'Marriage Group'.

It does not seem, then, from a survey of the structural relationship of these seven tales that to present anything like a group of stories dealing with marriage was Chaucer's intention. An examination of the content of the seven tales is no more indicative of the existence of such a group. Here I have space to examine only one of them, the *Wife of Bath's Tale*, from this point of view. Her *Prologue* is a masterly piece of work, portraying a woman obsessed by her theory of woman's sovereignty in marriage; but she is so mesmerized by her subject that she seems to miss the moral of her own story:

> And thus they lyve unto hir lyves ende   *their*
> In parfit joye; and Jhesu Crist us sende
> Housbondes meeke, yonge, and fressh abedde,
> And grace t'overbyde hem that we wedde;   *dominate*
> And eek I praye Jhesu shorte hir lyves
> That wol nat be governed by hir wyves;
> And olde and angry nygardes of dispence,   *misers*
> God sende hem soone verray pestilence!
> CT: WIFE OF BATH'S TALE III, 1257-64

In the tale itself, a knight is set the task of finding out what it is that every woman wants. At the last minute an old hag tells him the answer; the price of this turns out to be to marry her. She tries to alleviate this not very enticing situation by giving him the choice of having her old and faithful or young and unfaithful. Faced with this awkward dilemma he puts the choice in her hands:

'Thanne have I gete of yow maistrie,' quod she,
'Syn I may chese and governe as me lest?'   *as it pleases me*
'Ye, certes, wyf,' quod he, 'I holde it best.'
                                    CT: WIFE OF BATH'S TALE III, 1236–8

It would thus appear that the knight took the Wife of Bath's advice, and as a result they lived happily ever after 'in parfit joye'. The only thing against this interpretation is that it is proved wrong in the twenty lines between these two quotations. Once he had given her the choice in one thing, the hag returns everything into his hands; she becomes both young and faithful:

... And she obeyed hym in every thyng
That myghte doon hym plesance or likyng.
                                    CT: WIFE OF BATH'S TALE III, 1255–6

In fact, the situation is like that in the *Franklin's Tale*, where Dorigen and Arveragus live happily in mutual respect; it is not at all like the Wife of Bath and her henpecked husbands. It begins to look as if what women want is their husband's love, not his obedience. It is love that the hag really wants; and so in fact does the Wife of Bath herself. On her own admission she was happier with Jannekin, who loved her and treated her roughly, than with the older husbands whom she was able to terrorize: 'In bacon hadde I nevere delit.' That is, she preferred her men young, not old and dried. Part at least of the humour of the *Wife of Bath's Tale* comes from the ironic contrast between what she preaches and her heart-felt, though perhaps unconscious, beliefs. Chaucer is very much alive to the dramatic possibilities of the bombshell the Wife introduces, but he is more likely to work in more subtle ways—by pricking the bubble of the Wife's enthusiasm—than by introducing a large-scale set debate.

THE IMPORTANCE OF THE LINKS

But whatever the rights and wrongs of the 'Marriage Group' question, Chaucer probably intended us to see the tales as a connected whole, hence the interest of the various prologues and links. It is in the interplay of character—Miller and Reeve, Host and Pardoner, Clerk and Wife of Bath—that Chaucer shows himself the observer of ordinary human nature; it is here that he becomes what we would now call a novelist, a portrayer of real life—as Fielding is, or Jane Austen, or Dickens (indeed more so, perhaps, than Dickens). It is a pity that most people (having studied Chaucer at school) have read only the *General Prologue* to the *Canterbury Tales* and perhaps one or two tales, often without the appropriate links; for then they get no idea of the liveliness and vigour of Chaucer's portrayal of human nature. The *Prologue* by itself merely presents the figures; they begin to move and breathe and quarrel only in the last few lines; and they come to life fully only in the course of the journey as they react to each other's tales. This is the best of Chaucer, by modern standards.

THE CHARACTERS AND THEIR TALES

To say this, however, is not to belittle the tales themselves, only to correct a partial view of the merits of the *Canterbury Tales*. The tales are, of course, worth reading for their own sake. They are drawn from many sources, and if they are not entirely original that is something the Middle Ages would consider a virtue, not a blemish. This may complicate the linking of the teller and the tale, especially as some of the tales antedate the collection as a whole, but there are few obvious mismatches—the female narrator of the *Shipman's Tale* is the most notorious example—and also few indissoluble connections between the teller and the tale. The Wife of Bath and the Canon's Yeoman let their hair down in their prologues, but it is the Pardoner alone whose tale is absolutely in character and closely welded to his prologue (see pp. 150–1). The Knight tells a knightly romance in a courtly style; his son, the Squire, follows suit. The Second Nun tells a typical saint's legend, and her superior, the Prioress, shows that the love emblazoned on her badge is, for the moment, divine not secular as she tells the miraculous story of the martyrdom of a young choirboy. In general, also, the 'cherls' tend to tell 'cherls' tales', though accuracy of characterization does not extend to making the Miller's drunkenness, which thrusts him forward, prevent him from telling smoothly and without a hitch a highly complicated story.

It is these 'cherls' tales' that have the most appeal today both because of their content, which tends towards the indecent, and their style, which is economical and realistic. The Miller, Reeve, Cook (though only a fragment exists of his tale) and Shipman, together with the Friar and Summoner, tell tales after the style of the medieval French *fabliau*. The *fabliau* is characterized by a spareness and directness of plot and expression: description is kept to the functional—few objects are singled out that are not used in the plot later on. Furthermore, these items tend toward the everyday, the homely and the practical. The characters are bourgeois or lower class, and many of them are rascals of one sort or another. The *fabliau*, as the name might suggest, is French in origin, and these tales are almost the only English versions extant. This and the fact that such a large proportion of the tales are in this *genre* seems to suggest that Chaucer's interest was so captured by the French versions that he experimented with the form, and attempted to widen the range of court poetry by introducing bourgeois elements. Perhaps this new interest was the cause of his never finishing the *Legend of Good Women*.

To the simple *fabliau*, however, Chaucer added his own touches. The narrative, though still fast, has more time for descriptions of the setting, but more particularly of the people. This is certainly true of the *Miller's Tale*, which is one of the more fully developed examples of Chaucer's *fabliaux*. The scene is soon set; it is Oxford where a rich old carpenter, John by name, boards students from the university. At the moment he has a poor student who has turned his attention to astrology. He is something of a dark horse; he is an expert in the conduct of secret affairs. Next we learn that John has just married an eighteen-year-old wife, whom he guards jealously, and well he might, for she is very beautiful and high-spirited too. She is described at length, just as Blanche is in the *Book of the Duchess*, but with a difference; these are not the old stock phrases of the courtly romances that Chaucer uses but similes using the down-to-earth objects of the *fabliau*:

> Fair was this yonge wyf, and therwithal
> As any wezele hir body gent and smal.   *slender*
> A ceynt she werede, barred al of silk,   *belt   striped*
> A barmclooth eek as whit as morne milk   *apron*
> Upon hir lendes, ful of many a goore.   *loins   pleat*
>
> . . . .
> She was ful moore blisful on to see
> Than is the newe pere-jonette tree,   *early pear*
> And softer than the wolle is of a wether.
>
> . . . .
> She was a prymerole, a piggesnye,   *primrose   cuckoo flower*
> For any lord to leggen in his bedde,   [(lit. *pig's eye*)
> Or yet for any good yeman to wedde.

CT. MILLER'S TALE I, 3233–70

It is almost as if Chaucer was making fun of the stilted style of the romances by introducing homely material and organizing it in the traditional way.

Nicholas and Alison (for these are the names of the student and the wife) soon fall in love and come to an understanding, whereupon a second contestant appears upon the scene. He is the dandified Absolon, who combines the offices of parish clerk and barber. He cuts a rather ridiculous figure in his finery, somewhat like Malvolio in his cross-gartered stockings; but Alison is not to be moved by his protestations of love: as she tells John, there is no need for him to be jealous over Absolon's serenade—she loves another.

Now, with the scene set and the characters introduced, the farce begins. Nicholas retires to his room for a day or so, until John is worried by his absence and sends his servant upstairs (observe the little details):

> An hole he foond, ful lowe upon a bord,
> Ther as the cat was wont in for to crepe,
> And at that hole he looked in ful depe,
> And at the laste he had of hym a sight.

This Nicholas sat evere capyng upright,   *staring*
As he had kiked on the newe moone.   *looked at*

CT: MILLER'S TALE I, 3440-5

On being roused, Nicholas discloses what has been troubling
him, and persuades John that his science has shown him that there
is going to be a repeat performance of Noah's flood the next
week. The three of them must take refuge in tubs hung in the
rafters, ready to cut themselves adrift when the flood comes.
Alison and John must be in separate tubs,

> . . . For that bitwixe yow shal be no synne,
> Namoore in lookyng than ther shal in deede.   3590-1

When night comes, however, the two lovers descend from their
tubs and happily settle down to spend the rest of the night
together in sin, while John snores on in the roof beams. In the
course of the remainder of this not uneventful night, Absolon
appears again and is tricked into kissing Alison's buttocks in
mistake for her cheek, but when Nicholas tries to work the
same trick for Absolon's second visit he finds himself branded
with a red-hot coulter, the instrument of Absolon's revenge.
His cry for water for his burnt backside wakes John, who thinks
that Noah's flood has come, and cuts himself loose; as a result he
ends up in the cellar with a broken arm, and Nicholas and Alison
have little difficulty in persuading the neighbours, brought in
by the commotion, that John is mad.

Throughout the tale each new development is prepared for
in advance; the remark that John takes in lodgers prepares the
way for Nicholas two lines later; the latter's astrological leanings
prepare for the plot to deceive John; his propensity for women,
his love for Alison. John's unwise marriage:

> He knew nat Catoun, for his wit was rude,
> That bad man sholde wedde his simylitude.   *likeness*
> Men sholde wedden after hire estaat,
> For youthe and elde is often at debaat.

CT: MILLER'S TALE I, 3227-30

prepares the way for his eventual downfall. Absolon's singing leads up to his serenade, and his serenade acquaints us with the fateful window that is to play its part at the dénouement. In this sort of way the whole story is tied together. This careful construction is one of the points that show its ancestry is to be sought in the *fabliau*; though the *Miller's Tale* is richer by far than most *fabliaux* in its descriptive techniques, it is still fully in their tradition. Their use of detail is the same as in Chaucer's own realistic style, and the mingling of Chaucer's humour with the *fabliau* approach gives us a new richness of comic tale, of which the *Miller's Tale* is a first-rate example.

THE FOLK TALE: THE 'NUN'S PRIEST'S TALE'

About a quarter of the *Canterbury Tales* as we have them are *fabliaux*; about the same proportion have their origins in the folk tale. The Man of Law's tale of Constance, the Wife of Bath's tale of the Loathly Bride, the Clerk's tale of patient Griselda, the Merchant's Pear Tree episode and the Tell Tale Bird all have a folk tale as their basis. Some seem to have come directly from the reservoir of folk memory, others via other writers: the Clerk, as befits a learned man, takes his from Petrarch, and the Manciple from Ovid. Like the *fabliaux*, these are told with a directness and freshness—but without the bawdiness. Moreover the plot, being well-known, is often used merely as a vehicle for Chaucer's humour.

The *Nun's Priest's Tale* is one of these, and perhaps the finest example of Chaucer's humour at work. Here he has taken a trivial episode, the well-known story of how a cock was beguiled by a fox's flattery and escaped by playing on his captor's pride, but the treatment is in the epic manner, and the whole tale is an exercise in the humour of the incongruous, which is the essence of the mock-heroic. Chaucer's technique is that of the banana skin: we start upon some flight of rhetoric only to be brought down to earth with a bump when we realize that the scene is a farmyard and the actors only hens. This banana skin is there ready for anyone who tries to take the poem too seriously. Admittedly, it is a comic poem and admittedly it is packed with exaggerated rhetorical devices, but this is no reason to suppose Chaucer was intending to ridicule the established way of padding meagre material which he himself does constantly, any more than he is indicting dream or astrological theory. The humour rather lies in the incongruity of style and place: a farmyard is no place for the high style; such activities as go on there are beneath the notice of well-bred people and should be told in low style.

The background is sketched in the opening lines: there was a poor widow living in a small cottage in a wooded valley; she is so poor that she is almost below the bread line, but in her yard is a magnificent cock called Chauntecleer (clear singer) whose splendour appears all the more striking in contrast to the meanness of his surroundings. His description recalls all the lavishness of chivalric romance—even his comb is

> . . . batailled as it were a castel wal;
> His byle was blak, and as the jeet it shoon;   *bill*
> Lyk asure were his legges and his toon;
> His nayles whitter than the lylye flour
> And lyk the burned gold was his colour.
>
> CT: NUN'S PRIEST'S TALE VII, 2860–4 (B4050–4)

The next line reminds us where we are:

> This gentil cok hadde in his governaunce
> Sevene hennes   2865

and adds an incongruity of its own: a cock may indeed be well-bred, but not in the sense of *gentil*, with its connotations of a different sort of breeding, of knighthood and courtesy—we are reminded of the '. . . verray parfit gentil knyght' of the *Prologue*.

There follows a long argument with his favourite wife, Pertelote, about the origin and significance of dreams. She holds that they are the result of a functional disorder of the humours, and, full of wifely concern, urges a laxative upon him; he is sure that they foretell the future, and quotes a string of learned examples from Cicero onwards to prove his point. Then after this long episode of learned human discourse we are brought back with a bump:

> And with that word he fley doun fro the beem,
> For it was day, and eke his hennes alle,

And with a chuk he gan hem for to calle,
For he hadde founde a corn, lay in the yerd.

CT: NUN'S PRIEST'S TALE VII, 3172-5 (B4362-5)

Now as the fox breaks in, the style rises yet higher:

O false mordrour, lurkynge in thy den!
O newe Scariot, newe Genylon,   *Judas*
False dissymulour, o Greek Synon,   *traitor*
That broughtest Troye al outrely to sorwe!   *utterly*
O Chauntecleer, accursed be that morwe
That thou into that yerd flaugh fro the bemes!

CT: NUN'S PRIEST'S TALE 3226-31 (B4416-21)

And again at the fateful moment of Chauntecleer's downfall:

O destinee, that mayst nat been eschewed!   *avoided*
Allas, that Chauntecleer fleigh fro the bemes!
Allas, his wyf ne roghte nat of dremes!   *cared not for*
And on a Friday fil al this meschaunce.

CT: NUN'S PRIEST'S TALE 3338-41 (B4528-31)

—an apostrophe which is backed up by an appeal to the master
of medieval rhetoric, Geoffroy de Vinsauf. But the heroic style
of the lamentations, which are not in fact far removed from
those of the *Troilus* and the *Franklin's Tale*, is suddenly shattered
by the low farce of the chase, which is unfortunately too long
to quote in full. Suffice it to say that the personnel involved is
in itself an uproarious mixture, and the noise must have been
terrific:

Ran Colle oure dogge, and Talbot and Gerland,
And Malkyn, with a dystaf in hir hand;
Ran cow and calf, and eek the verray hogges,
So fered for the berkyng of the dogges
And shoutyng of the men and wommen eeke,
They ronne so hem thoughte hir herte breeke.
They yolleden as feendes doon in helle;   *yelled*
The dokes cryden as men wolde hem quelle;   *kill*
The gees for feere flowen over the trees;
Out of the hyve cam the swarm of bees.

CT: NUN'S PRIEST'S TALE 3383-92 (B4573-82)

Suddenly, however, we are back to serious matters:

> Now, goode men, I prey yow herkneth alle:
> Lo, how Fortune turneth sodeynly
> The hope and pryde eek of hir enemy!
>
> CT: NUN'S PRIEST'S TALE 3402–4 (B4592)

and we finish with a moral and the usual prayer.

THE 'PARDONER'S TALE'

As I said earlier, the *Pardoner's Tale* stands alone in its exploitation of the character of its teller. It is a confession rather than a story, and a boast rather than a confession. The Pardoner is one of the more unsavoury of the pilgrims, and yet he has one of the best stories: this may be thought to lend weight to my earlier suggestion that Chaucer found vice more interesting than virtue, and was experimenting in widening the scope of upper-class literature by making the *fabliau* and similar folk *genres* acceptable.

One might perhaps have expected the Pardoner to tell an indecent story in the same vein as his companion the Summoner. So did the pilgrims:

> But right anon thise gentils gonne to crye,
> 'Nay, lat him telle us of no ribaudye!   *ribaldry*
> Telle us som moral thyng, that we may leere   *learn*
> Som wit, and thanne wol we gladly heere.'
>
> CT: PARDONER'S HEADLINK VI, 323–6

He has now no choice but to tell a 'moral tale'; and unless he prepares his ground very carefully his story will be too much at variance with his obvious way of life, and he will be exposed. This is why he reveals his methods. If he is to be shown up as a rogue, he may as well show *himself* up and appear as a clever rogue. Thus the *Prologue* to his tale is not at all out of character, as some critics have suggested. He makes clear his motives in preaching—that he is in it for the money; he tells us of his drink and women, so that when he starts his sample sermon, both we and the pilgrims themselves (for this is a story within a story) can enjoy the irony of an avaricious lecher preaching eloquently against lechery and avarice. He is a splendid preacher—after all, he makes a good living by his tongue. As he says himself, he has a successful technique:

> Thanne peyne I me to strecche forth the necke,
> And est and west upon the peple I bekke,
> As dooth a dowve sittynge on a berne.   *barn*
> Myne handes and my tonge goon so yerne   *move so eagerly*
> That it is joye to se my bisynesse.
> Of avarice and of swich cursednesse
> Is al my prechyng, for to make hem free
> To yeven hir pens, and namely unto me.   *especially*
>
> CT: PARDONER'S PROL. VI, 395–402

So it is no surprise that the kernel of his sermon, his *exemplum* or warning example, is exquisitely told. It is the story of how three young men-about-town find death unawares in a pile of gold coins. It has been called the finest short story in the English language; no analysis can do it justice, and I am not going to attempt one. The power and solemnity of the story is somewhat diminished, however, by his final appeal to his supposed audience, after which—by a masterstroke of Chaucer's—he turns to the actual audience, the pilgrims, and adds his concluding prayer:

> And lo, sires, thus I preche.
> And Jhesu Crist, that is oure soules leche,   *physician*
> So graunte yow his pardoun to receyve,
> For that is best; I wol yow nat deceyve.
>
> CT: PARDONER'S TALE VI, 915–8

Had he stopped there all might have been well, but quite as an afterthought he over-reaches himself by jokingly inviting the pilgrims to come and buy his pardons; and his downfall comes with the brutal rejoinder of the Host, Harry Bailey.

CONCLUSION: '*Writen for oure doctrine*'

Even the rascally Pardoner's thoughts turn to the eternal verities at the end of his tale; so too at the end of *Troilus and Criseyde* Chaucer placed the whole story in the perspective of Divine Love. We may feel that these pious endings jar a little; but in an age when the Church had an all-embracing role in people's lives, and when the fear of damnation was real and universal, they were only to be expected. In the words of the Parson, whose very moral tract comes at the end of the *Canterbury Tales*:

> And he that synneth and verraily [*truly*] repenteth hym in his laste, hooly chirche yet hopeth his savacioun, by the grete mercy of oure Lord Jhesu Crist, for his repentaunce. . . .
>
> CT: PARSON'S TALE X, 93

As is clear from the *Prologue*, the Parson is an image of the Good Shepherd; he is

> . . . a lerned man, a clerk,
> That Cristes gospel trewely wolde preche.
>
> CT: GEN. PROL. I, 480–1

Thus his tale, a sermon on penitence, cannot be thought an artistic failure, as moderns who are bored by sermons make out. Given the premise that 'al that is writen is writen for oure doctrine', and the corollary that any writing that is not dedicated to the greater glory of God is *ipso facto* sinful, he could hardly have told a tale in the worldly style of most of the other pilgrims. Still, what may jar a little is the Parson's promise, in his *Prologue*:

> . . . I wol yow telle a myrie tale in prose
> To knitte up al this feeste, and make an ende.   *sum up*
> And Jhesu, for his grace, wit me sende
> To shewe yow the wey, in this viage,
> Of thilke parfit glorious pilgrymage
> That highte Jerusalem celestial.
>
> CT: PARSON'S PROL. X, 46–51

He certainly fulfils the second part of this promise, but modern taste would hardly agree with his description of the tale as *merry*. However, we must remember that both words and tastes change. The sale of books of sermons as recently as the last century was enormous, and we have already seen—how could a reader of Chaucer forget?—that words change their meanings. If we were to understand by *myrie* something like *pleasant*, we would come near the Parson's intentions.

Granted, then, that the *Parson's Tale* and *Prologue* are not out of place, some may still feel that Chaucer's *Retraction*, with which he ends the *Canterbury Tales*, is out of character, and even downright hypocritical. Some have thought it spurious, a pious gesture of a monkish copyist and not Chaucer's work at all. Taking his leave of his readers, he says:

> . . . preye for me that Crist have mercy on me and foryeve me my giltes[*sins*]; and namely [*especially*] of my translacions and enditynges [*writing*] of worldly vanitees, the whiche I revoke in my retracciouns; as is the book of Troilus; the book also of Fame; the book of the xxv Ladies [*Legend of Good Women*]; the book of the Duchesse; the book of Seint Valentynes day of the Parlement of Briddes; the tales of Caunterbury, thilke that sownen into synne; the book of the Leoun; and many another book, if they were in my remembraunce, and many a song and many a leccherous lay; that Crist for his grete mercy foryeve me the synne.
>
> CT: PARSON'S TALE X, 1083

To call this insincere is to argue against the temper of the times, to imagine that someone whose work is in many ways so modern had a 20th-century mind imprisoned in a 14th-century body. To us moderns, the works he mentions are quite innocuous, but the love they celebrate is human, not divine, and hence, strictly speaking, they are sinful because they are not 'writen for oure doctrine'. It is not for us to impose our 20th-century standards, and to expect Chaucer to put in his *Retraction* for form's sake, and then like Galileo to turn away, muttering under his breath, 'Eppur si muove' (but it *does* move). Let us be thankful that it is merely a retraction, and not an actual destruction of these works. It is no doubt a compliment to Chaucer's skill that we should think the retraction out of character; but maybe we would get more from his work if we were to approach it on his terms and not our own.

It is to help the reader to do this that this book has been written.

9

Chaucer's Reputation

Each age puts its own interpretation on the literature of the past. To us, of course, our predecessors' views will often appear partial, and sometimes plain wrong. Chaucer has been praised for many things at different times, and if we do not agree, this ought to warn us that the current interpretation may be no less partial than those of the past.

His contemporaries and immediate successors praised him for his technical skill. He was a poet learned in the art of rhetoric, who first beautified and enhanced the English language. As Hoccleve said soon after Chaucer's death, he was 'the first findere of our faire langage'; and he embellished it until it was fit for polite society by introducing to the vernacular the teachings of the rhetoricians. The modern counterpart of this view and the one expounded in this book sees Chaucer beginning his career by adapting the familiar style of French courtly poetry to make English poetry acceptable to a French-orientated Court, and throughout his life gradually widening his range until in the *Canterbury Tales* he introduces the middle-class *fabliau* to polite society. The contemporary recognition of his 'improvement' of English is a confirmation of the current modern view that his work is not fairly represented when looked at as divided into 'periods'—an Italian period, a French period, and so on.

Later on, after the Reformation, Chaucer was first cast in the role of social critic, and enrolled among the ranks of the reformers. One authority (Foxe in his *Ecclesiastical History*, 1570) claimed that he was a follower of Wycliffe. Suffice it to say that there is no evidence for this either in his works or in what we know of his life.

By the time of Dryden, when the heroic couplet had so refined English verse, not unnaturally Chaucer's verse seemed rough and uncouth (Dryden was, of course, unaware of the theory of sounding the final -*e*, and actually contradicted an editor of Chaucer who propounded this notion). He had the grace to admit that 'there is the sweetness of a Scotch tune in it, which is natural and pleasing, though not perfect'. This Dryden attempted to amend by translating him into smooth heroic couplets. He also drew attention to Chaucer's character-drawing; the pilgrims, he said, were men and women whose descendants could still be seen.

From then on, the emphasis was upon his humour and his humanity, while difficulties with his language and verse become less important when he is no longer judged by the strict metrical rules of the 18th century. Coleridge, for instance, with his usual perception, took unceasing delight in him and found no difficulties with the verse or language. Hazlitt found in Chaucer a love of Nature, enrolling him, as it were, in the newly-founded Romantic School. Leigh Hunt, again, lays stress on his humour.

But the most famous dictum of the 19th century is Matthew Arnold's vintage Victorian judgement that 'something is wanting, which poetry must have before it can be placed in the glorious class of the best'. What is lacking is 'the high and excellent seriousness, which Aristotle assigns as one of the grand virtues of poetry'. This is an often-quoted remark which has received more attention than it deserves. Either Arnold in some strange Victorian way has equated seriousness with solemnity—and Chaucer is rarely solemn even at his most affecting—or else in his reading of Chaucer he never encountered *Troilus and Criseyde* and in particular the closing stanzas, or even the *Prioress's Tale* from the *Canterbury Tales*. He consequently put Chaucer below Homer, Dante and Shakespeare, and in doing so frightened off the critics, and left the field open to the scholars.

Certainly at the end of the last century and the beginning of this, attention turned to fact-grubbing. The Chaucer Society combed the Public Records Office and other sources for mentions of Chaucer, and published quite a sizeable volume. This search has continued to the present day: a volume, even larger and more lavish, arrived from Texas a year before this one appeared in print. Another school, under the leadership of Kittredge, attempted to find the life records of the pilgrims—or at least of people who could have served as models for them. This is a fascinating exercise in detection, but hardly relevant to a critical appreciation of the poems.

A third set of hunters has tracked down the sources of Chaucer's tales. This work is more important, for if we can compare an original tale with Chaucer's version of it, and can be sure that this is the version that he used, we have a valuable insight into the way in which he worked, and a clue as to his intentions. The result of this line of research is Bryan and Dempster's *Sources and Analogues*.

Finally, work on the text of the *Canterbury Tales* culminated in Manly's monumental edition of 1940.

After this period of scholarly detective work, the emphasis has swung back to criticism, which can now rest on surer foundations. There is, however, a remarkable diversity of critical opinion, which does not make it easy to present a comprehensive picture. On the one wing are the anthropologists, who would read all medieval literature by the standards of *The Golden Bough*, and who think that to show that a story has its origins in a pagan ritual thereby explains it for us. On the other are the allegorists, who apply medieval theories of biblical explication to secular literature, and thereby seek to prove that the *fabliau* carries the same essential message as the Scriptures. Between these two extremes comes a larger body of saner opinion. Of these critics I find those the most convincing who attempt to read Chaucer in the light of his own times and world picture: while we cannot discount the effect his works have on our modern minds just because we *are* modern, it is also fruitful to see what meaning they had for his contemporaries.

But it is a truism that one volume of text is worth a dozen times its weight in criticism. The more pedestrian among us—and scholars are often pedestrian—cannot help but make literature appear pedestrian, too. Scholars earn their living by scholarship; where is the virtue in their labours if all they are doing is reading something that is actually enjoyable? Therefore, let my final advice to you be to read what Chaucer wrote rather than what other people think he wrote. Ten to one, they haven't any secret information—no hot line to the other world. And that goes for this book, too. If you have turned to the last pages to see how it all ends, start with Chaucer rather than this book. If you do, you may be surprised and delighted—Chaucer is often funny—and you will be in a better position to tell whether the rest of us are talking sense about him.

Bibliography

A select list of books that may be helpful is:

1. TEXTS

The best buy (though expensive) is still:

> *The Complete Works of Geoffrey Chaucer*; edited by F. N. Robinson. 2nd ed. (O.U.P., 1957).

Some individual Canterbury Tales have been edited by Maurice Hussey, A. C. Spearing and James Winney in the series *Selected Tales of Chaucer* (C.U.P., 1965–).

2. CRITICISM, ETC.

A. C. Baugh: *A History of the English Language*, 2nd ed. (Routledge, 1959).

H. S. Bennett: *Chaucer and the Fifteenth Century* (Clarendon Press, 1947).

H. S. Bennett: *Life on the English Manor* (C.U.P., 1937 PB).

D. S. Brewer: *Chaucer*, 2nd ed. (Longmans, 1960).

D. S. Brewer: *Chaucer in his Time* (Nelson, 1964).

W. F. Bryan and G. Dempster: *Sources and Analogues of Chaucer's Canterbury Tales* (Chicago U.P., 1941).

W. Clemen: *Chaucer's Early Poetry* (Methuen, 1964).

N. Coghill: *Geoffrey Chaucer* (Writers and their Work, 79) (Longmans, 1956 PB).

M. M. Crow and C. C. Olson (Eds.): *Chaucer Life Records*, 2nd ed. (Clarendon Press, 1966).

W. C. Curry: *Chaucer and the Medieval Sciences*, 2nd ed. (Allen and Unwin, 1960).

B. Ford (Ed.): *Pelican Guide to English Literature*. Vol. 1: *The Age of Chaucer* (Penguin Books, 1954 PB).

Hussey, Spearing and Winney: *An Introduction to Chaucer* (C.U.P., 1965).

H. Kökeritz: *A Guide to Chaucer's Pronunciation* (Holt, Rinehart and Winston, 1962 PB).

C. S. Lewis: *Allegory of Love* (Clarendon Press, 1936; repr. as Galaxy Book, 1958 PB).

C. S. Lewis: *The Discarded Image* (C.U.P., 1964).

J. L. Lowes: *Geoffrey Chaucer* (Clarendon Press, 1944).

F. Mossé: *Handbook of Middle English*; trans. James A. Walker (Johns Hopkins Press, 1952).

C. Muscatine: *Chaucer and the French Tradition* (California U.P., 1957 PB).

D. W. Robertson: *A Preface to Chaucer* (Princeton U.P., 1963).

J. G. Southworth: *Verses of Cadence: Assessment of Chaucer's Prosody* (Blackwell, 1954).

J. G. Southworth: *The Prosody of Chaucer and his Followers*: supplementary chapters to *Verses of Cadence* (Blackwell, 1962).

J. Speirs: *Chaucer the Maker*, 2nd ed. (Faber, 1962 PB).

Some of the important articles in periodicals have been reprinted in two paperback collections:

R. J. Schoeck and J. Taylor: *Chaucer Criticism*, 2 vols. (Notre Dame U.P. 1960–1).

E. Wagenknecht: *Chaucer: Modern Essays in Criticism* (Galaxy Books; O.U.P., 1959).

Index

Under *Canterbury Tales*, bold type has been used to indicate the pages on which the character of the narrator has been discussed rather than the actual tale.